Tales of the Night Sky

Retold by
Corinna Keefe

Illustrated by
Gaby Verdooren

This edition published in 2024 by Arcturus Publishing Limited
26/27 Bickels Yard, 151–153 Bermondsey Street,
London SE1 3HA

Copyright © Arcturus Holdings Limited

All rights reserved. No part of this publication may be reproduced, stored in a retrieval system, or transmitted, in any form or by any means, electronic, mechanical, photocopying, recording, or otherwise, without prior written permission in accordance with the provisions of the Copyright Act 1956 (as amended). Any person or persons who do any unauthorized act in relation to this publication may be liable to criminal prosecution and civil claims for damages.

Author: Corinna Keefe
Illustrator: Gaby Verdooren
Editor: Becca Clunes
Designer: Allie Oldfield
Design Manager: Rosie Bellwood-Moyler
Managing Editor: Joe Harris

ISBN: 978-1-3988-3890-1
CH011947NT
Supplier 29, Date 1024, PI 00007712

Printed in China

CONTENTS

Introduction 4

Atahensic Lands on Earth 9
Based on Iroquois Native American myths

The Weaver Girl and the Herdsman 16
Based on a Chinese tale

The Buried Moon 24
Based on a traditional German story

Tama-rereti Goes Fishing 32
Based on Maori myths

Sol and Skoll 40
Based on Norse myths

The Feathered Serpent and the Moon Rabbit 48
Based on an Aztec tale

The Little Girl with a Big Voice 56
Based on South African stories

Aglaonike Catches the Moon 65
Based on Greek myths

Evening Star and Orphan Star 72
Based on a Caddo Native American tale

Hina and the Shark 80
Based on Tongan myths

How Fisher Brought the Sun to Earth 88
Based on an Ojibwa Native American folktale

How Thoth Won the Moon 96
Based on Egyptian myths

Lindu and the Northern Lights 104
Based on a traditional Estonian folktale

The Man Who Made the Sun 112
Based on a Diné Native American story

The Seven Sisters and the Bear 120
Based on a Kiowa Native American folktale

INTRODUCTION

Most of us know more about the daytime sky than the sky at night. During the day, we notice all its changes: blue sky, clouds, rain, snow, and the way the wind moves everything about. But we're less familiar with the night sky. It's so big and dark! Doesn't it all look the same?

In fact, the night sky has many secrets to reveal. It might be darker, but its darkness ranges from pitch-black to dark purples, and soft blues. Before the sun comes up, dawn is preceded by tiny, second-by-second changes in hue as the sky begins to lighten. Clouds glitter as they pass across the Moon. And of course, there are the stars, from the spark of distant planets to the flowing river of the Milky Way.

People in the past were much more used to the night sky. To begin with, they didn't have the constant electric light or air pollution that we're used to today. They relied on fires and candles or simply their own eyesight. They knew that some nights would be easier to explore than others as the Moon grew larger, while a few nights each month would be almost completely dark.

They could read the night sky like a map. There are still some people who have this skill today, but it's less common. If you know what you are doing, you can use the stars to find North and chart a path to your destination. You might even figure out the rough time and season from looking at the Moon.

Navigation is not the only use for the night sky. For thousands of years, the sky at night has also been a source of stories. Scary stories, exciting stories, romantic stories, stories about adventures, giants, animals, battles, hunting, cooking, weaving, monsters, lovers, children, families, games, and riddles.

Some of the stories are very old, like the ancient Egyptian tale of why the Moon changes size every month. Versions of that story may have been told for around 5,000 years. Even the stories that are not quite that old have been around for hundreds of years.

It's incredible that those stories are still being told today. The Ancient Egyptians are buried in their pyramids, the Vikings haven't sailed their ships since the eleventh century,

and the Aztec empire fell in the sixteenth century. But the myths and legends that they told each other are still around. That means that people have passed down their stories, either spoken or written, again and again.

Probably some of the details have become mixed up. Every time a story gets told, it changes a little bit, even if the person telling the story didn't mean to do it. I've borrowed and retold these stories from all over the world, so I have probably changed them, too, but I've tried to keep the spirit of each tale the same.

Why have these stories lasted for so long? In some cases, it's because they explain something about how the night sky works.

The story of the Weaver Girl and the Herdsman explains why the Milky Way appears brighter at certain times of the year. Fisher's story explains why the Earth is so much darker and colder in winter. Around the world, lots of people have noticed that the marks on the Moon look a bit like a rabbit, so the tale of Quetzalcoatl's adventures explains how the jackrabbit got there. In the twenty-first century, we have scientific explanations for these things as well, but we still enjoy the stories.

Another interesting way to think about the night sky is to compare it with the daytime. We see the importance of the Sun in stories such as The Man Who Made the Sun or Sol and Skoll.

However, I don't think that we have stories just to explain what we see. We also tell stories about who we want to be. The little girl with the big voice, the lost boy who stands up against evil, and the courageous seven sisters are all ordinary people who do amazing things.

Some of the stories are also there to remind us what *not* to do—like the three friends who bury the Moon or the witch who thought she was more important than a Moon goddess. It turns out that it's usually a bad idea to mess with the night sky.

I hope you will enjoy reading these legends and find inspiration in them. Some of the characters you will meet in this book have been around for longer than the pyramids, so you can be sure that they have good stories to tell.

ATAHENSIC Lands on EARTH

Based on Iroquois Native American myths

This is a story from the time when the Universe was a very new idea. The sky was still filling up with blue, and the Earth was still soft and crumbly, like a cookie that's just come out of the oven.

The only plants and animals at that time all lived in the sea. The seaweed was growing a mile a day, and all the creatures were sprouting exciting new features. The beavers were learning how to chew, the otters practiced their dives and corkscrew turns, and the turtle popped its head in and out of its shell a hundred times a day to get used to the motion.

Far up above, the stars watched everything that was happening from their seats in the sky. Among them was Atahensic, the Sky Woman of the Iroquois. She was young and brave, but she was very easily distracted. All day, she would sit and stare at the funny things happening on Earth and barely remember to shine any light.

"Pay attention! Your light's going out," the other stars would say to her, crossly.

"Atahensic, you must be more careful!" her father would say. "Are you listening to me, young lady?"

But Atahensic was busy watching the Earth. Muskrats had just been invented, and the first trees were having a competition to see how tall they could grow from their roots that floated in the ocean depths.

As time passed, the seas filled up with more and more wonderful creatures. Atahensic spent all day and night staring at the blue planet with her eyes open wide. What a grand new idea the Universe had been!

Then, one day, Atahensic's lack of attention got her into serious trouble.

The trees had been working hard to grow taller and stronger. Now one of them brushed against the Moon. Another twined its uppermost branches around the legs of Atahensic's chair. And one tree, more ambitious than all the rest, kept going. Up and up it went, past Atahensic, past the stars, out into the dark, undiscovered depths of space.

Then it began to sway and bow with its own colossal weight. There was a creaking noise, then a snapping noise, then a shrieking noise. The tree was falling! But Atahensic didn't notice. She was leaning forward in her chair, watching eagerly as a pod of dolphins swam by.

Slowly, the tree bent double and began to topple back toward Earth. The other stars shrieked and hid under their chairs. But still, Atahensic didn't notice.

The tree's branches shook, and it wavered back and forth across the sky. And finally, as it swept past one last time, it knocked Atahensic out of her chair.

Down she fell, tumbling and turning in the wake of the tree. The wind whistled past her face, and she saw the other stars' faces as shocked white blurs whipping past her.

Below, the tree finally reached Earth. It fell into the waters with an enormous splash and kept on going. It was so heavy that it sank straight down to the bottom of the ocean and smashed a hole through the Earth's soft, freshly cooked crust. That hole was deeper than the deepest well and wider than a blue whale from its nose to its tail.

Atahensic was distracted for a moment by watching the tree and how it sent waves crisscrossing all over the planet. Then she remembered that she was still falling, too, and she would make a splash herself when she crash-landed in the ocean. It was a long, long, long way down from where the stars sat to the Earth.

She had seen other stars fall before. They would blaze brighter than ever as they reached the ring of clouds around the Earth. She had watched in awe as they streaked across the sky—then flared and fizzled out just before they sank into the water.

She began to feel scared. Was she just imagining it, or was she already shining brighter? She tried to call out, but she was falling so fast that she couldn't pull the air into her lungs. She waved her arms, but it did nothing to slow her down.

The stars looked very far away now. She could feel the air growing warmer around her as she approached the Earth, and she could see tiny ripples on the surface of the ocean that had looked so smooth from above.

Then she heard another noise. At first, she thought it was just the rushing of the wind, but that wasn't quite right. The wind shrilled and whistled, but this sound was soft, like silken fabric. From time to time, she could hear a cheep, a squawk, and a flutter. Birds!

A great wave of seabirds rose up toward Atahensic, curving and circling through the sky. There were shearwaters and cormorants, kittiewakes and guillemots, gulls, terns, auks, and murres, skuas, and storm petrels, puffins and pelicans, frigate birds and fulmar, albatrosses, razorbills, and jaegers. They surrounded Atahensic on every side, calling out cheerfully. She stared in wonder as they flew around her, above her, and below, shielding her from the breeze and slowing her headlong descent. Their chatter calmed her down. She realized that she wasn't going to burn up, after all.

Atahensic floated down toward the Earth as light as a feather, cushioned by the outstretched wings of thousands of seabirds.

As the waves rushed up toward them, the birds began to sheer off one by one, returning to their patrol above the waves. Atahensic slipped gently into the salt water and waved them goodbye.

"Thank you! Thank you! Thank—oof!" she said, as she caught a mouthful of seawater.

There she was at last, kicking and gasping in the blue ocean that she had watched from space for so long. She was surprised by how cold it felt in real life and how big the waves were. She could feel them heaving around her, lifting her up then pouring her down, as if the Earth itself was breathing in and out in big, slow breaths.

She paddled her arms and turned in a circle, taking it all in. There were the dolphins, squeaking and calling to each other as they zipped through the water. There was a patch of kelp, reaching up through the sea with its beautiful long curls. And here were little fish, in all the hues of the rainbow, swimming around her; and here was a shark, long and silver-dark like an arrow; and here was an octopus, transparent as glass, pushing itself past her …

Without realizing it, Atahensic had already sunk very deep in the ocean. Her starlight shed just enough light for her to see all the wonderful plants and creatures. But even stars can't hold their breath forever.

Three little animals that had been splashing about near the surface had watched Atahensic fall. Now they were starting to worry.

"She sank awfully fast," said the beaver.

"I'm not sure she knows how to swim," observed the otter.

"But everybody knows how to swim!" said the muskrat. "Don't they?"

As the three of them paddled around in a circle, they watched the trail of bubbles rising up from where Atahensic had fallen. There was no sign of the beautiful star lady herself. Her light had long since disappeared into the depths.

"We ought to do something," said the otter, who was the smartest of them all.

"What if we built a nice dam?" suggested the beaver, looking excited. "We could stop the water just here, drain out that side, go down and fetch her …"

"It would have to be a very big dam," said the muskrat, nervously.

"No, I'm afraid that won't work at all," said the otter. "We're going to need a deep-sea expert. Hey! Turtle! You over there!"

The turtle looked up and swam lazily over to the three little animals.

"What's going on?" he said, in a big, deep voice.

Quickly, the otter explained how they had watched the tree fall, and how it had knocked Atahensic out of the sky and into the well that the tree had left in the Earth.

"… and we're pretty sure she can't swim," finished the otter. "Do you think you could go and fetch her?"

"No problem at all," said the turtle. "Wait here for a moment, please."

The turtle dived straight down, following the chain of bubbles that rose up from the bottom of the ocean. He flew quickly through the water as it deepened from gentle blue to twilight to the deep, black darkness of the farthest depths.

That was where he found Atahensic, almost at the bottom of the endless well left by the tree. It was a long journey even for a turtle, and he could feel his breath fading just as he finally caught sight of her.

"Atahensic!" he called out. "Sky Woman! Can you hear me? Grab hold of my shell!"

He swam underneath her, and Atahensic clung onto his shell with the tips of her fingers. Feeling that his strength was almost gone, the turtle swam desperately up toward the light.

Overhead, the muskrat, the otter, and the beaver were still circling the spot where the turtle had disappeared and Atahensic had fallen. The beaver kept chattering anxiously all the time.

"If only we had made a dam—except then, perhaps—well, maybe if we'd—I wonder if old Turtle—what if they—"

"Oh, do calm down," said the otter. "They'll be up here again in no time, you'll see."

But it felt like a very long wait until they finally saw the turtle's head break through the waves, with his beady eyes smiling and Atahensic riding on his back. She had almost completely recovered, although she was still slightly out of breath, and she was thrilled to have got a second look at all the ocean creatures.

"She's back! She's back!" cried the beaver. "I knew you'd make it, Turtle. Never a doubt in my mind."

"Welcome to Earth," the otter said politely, offering Atahensic one of her best rocks.

"Will you be staying long?" asked the muskrat, wistfully.

Atahensic looked up at the sky and thought what a long, long way away it was. So very far away from waves, and seaweed, and friends who gave you their best rocks, and fish that came in all the hues of the rainbow.

"I'd like to stay," she said shyly, "if there's any space for me."

"Well, about that," said the beaver. "I think I might have an idea."

He asked them all to collect seaweed, pieces of driftwood, tree branches, and even sand from the shallower reaches of the ocean. Under the beaver's careful direction, they built a huge raft with the turtle in the middle of it, so that Atahensic had a dry place to sit while they all roamed across the oceans together. That was the first island.

Atahensic lived a long and happy life on Earth. She saw every one of the seven seas and even came up with some useful ideas, like making even bigger islands, and making land animals, and growing plants for food. Sometimes, she missed the stars, but then she had the idea of having children, so that she could have new star friends on Earth. And that's how all of us are here today.

The Weaver Girl and the Herdsman

Based on a Chinese tale

Take a look out of the window. What can you see? If there are clouds sweeping across the sky, then the Weaver Girl Tchi-Niu must be hard at work.

Tchi-Niu is the daughter of the Sun. She sits at her loom, and nobody else can weave so finely as she does. From delicate little puffs of altocumulus, to the low, smooth drapes of stratus, the shimmer of cirrus, the soft cushions of cumulus, and the heavy stacks of cumulonimbus—Tchi-Niu weaves them all at her loom.

Her weaving frame stretches across the Moon. She dresses the frame each morning with strands of sunbeams, then weaves them through with long threads of raindrops. All the stars wear Tchi-Niu's cloth, because it is the best in the galaxy.

But the Weaver Girl isn't just renowned for her beautiful cloth. Rain falls from the clouds that she weaves across the sky, making the plants grow and giving people and animals water to drink. Perhaps today she'll leave you with a blue sky, but tomorrow she'll send rain to water the plants where you live.

There was a time, however, when Tchi-Niu neglected her duties. The Sun blazed

down on the Earth every day, the plants wilted, and the animals grew thirsty.

This is the story of how Tchi-Niu stopped weaving—and how she started again.

One day, many years ago, Tchi-Niu was hard at work. She was weaving a new tunic for her father, the Sun. She had carefully selected the reddest sunbeams, so that they would glow and glitter when he wore them, and beaded them with raindrops.

She often used to watch the stars while she worked. She liked to see the clothes that she had made. There went one star, shooting down to Earth in a beautiful cape; there went another, gliding sedately across the darkness of space in rainbow slippers.

But on this day, Tchi-Niu saw something that surprised her. *Twang!* Her hand slipped, and a thread of gold snapped. She sat staring at a strange new star.

You see, this star wasn't wearing any of Tchi-Niu's work. He was strolling along, wearing a battered straw hat, dusty old clothes, and shoes made out of oxskins.

"Excuse me!" called out Tchi-Niu. "Hey, you!"

But the Herdsman didn't hear her. Her voice was drowned out by the elegant white cattle that were trotting beside him.

She had to wait another week to see him again. None of the other stars seemed to know who he was. At last, she saw the white cattle meandering past her loom again, grazing on the short, sweet grasses of the Moon.

"Hello!" she called out. "Excuse me! I just wanted to ask you …"

This time, the Herdsman looked up, and Tchi-Niu saw his face for the first time.

She gasped and dropped her weaving. The Herdsman was the most beautiful star she had ever seen. His smooth black hair hung down over his deep brown eyes. His strong, tanned hands swung by his sides as he walked cheerfully across the sky.

He looked her straight in the eye—just for a second. Then he whistled to his cattle and turned aside.

"Wait! Come back!" said Tchi-Niu weakly. But it was too late. He had gone.

For the next few days, she could hardly concentrate at all. Who was the mysterious star? Why didn't he wear her clothes? And why wouldn't he talk to her?

After a while, Tchi-Niu's father, the Sun, dropped by to collect his new tunic.

"I'm sorry," she said, "I haven't finished it yet. You'll have to come back next week."

"What's taking so long?" asked her father. "A tunic like this only takes you a day."

She turned her face away and blushed.

"What is it, Tchi-Niu?" the Sun said, sternly. "I know something's going on. Come on, you can tell me."

Eventually, she confessed everything. She had fallen in love with the Herdsman, but she didn't even know his name.

"And," she explained, "I can't understand his clothes! Why hasn't he come to me for weaving before? Why won't he answer when I speak to him?"

"I think I know who you mean," said the Sun. "His name is Kien-Niou. He herds the cattle for the stars and brings us milk and butter. I suppose he's never needed your weaving because he wears the oxskins."

"But why won't he *talk* to me?" begged Tchi-Niu.

"Well, I suppose you haven't been introduced," said the Sun. "He's a very polite boy, you know. Very hardworking. Perhaps I could …"

"Oh, thank you, thank you, thank you!" said the Weaver Girl, dancing around the Sun for joy. "I'll have your tunic finished in half an hour!"

The Sun was concerned that his daughter had lost her heart too quickly. But he couldn't bear to see her unhappy—and besides, he wanted that new tunic. So he promised to fetch the Herdsman and introduce him to Tchi-Niu.

As soon as the two were introduced, they were the best of friends. Kien-Niou overcame his shyness, and Tchi-Niu got all the answers to her questions about the oxskins. (Even though, secretly, she was planning to weave him the softest cloak she could.)

The Herdsman began bringing his cattle past Tchi-Niu's loom every single day. The Weaver Girl neglected her other work to weave new clothes for Kien-Niou. Before long, it was clear to everyone that they were in love and would soon be married.

"Perhaps things will settle down then," said the Sun, looking ruefully at his socks, which were full of holes.

"Yesterday, all the cattle wandered off while he was busy staring at your daughter, and they started nibbling on the rings around my planet," said Jupiter, mournfully. "I can't take much more of this!"

When the day of the wedding came, all the stars and planets were there to celebrate. The Sun led the ceremony dressed in his best robes, which were only looking slightly threadbare. The heavenly cattle carried baskets of flowers on their backs and only tried to chew on the guests a couple of times. (Kien-Niou was too distracted to keep them in line.) Everybody agreed that it was a wonderful party, and soon the young lovers would be back to their normal routines.

But they were wrong. As time passed, Tchi-Niu and Kien-Niou only grew more in love. They could spend days at a time staring into each other's eyes. The Weaver Girl's loom stood empty, and the cattle roamed free across the sky.

The other stars began to complain. Their clothes were wearing thin. They hadn't had fresh milk or butter in weeks. Without the rain clouds, the Earth was so dry that the harvest failed.

"And I keep tripping over asteroids," said Venus, extremely irritated. "The cattle are supposed to graze them and keep them in check! This is intolerable."

"Something must be done," said Jupiter, and all the stars and planets looked pointedly at the Sun.

"All right, all right," he said wearily. "I'll see what I can do."

The Sun begged Tchi-Niu to return to her weaving.

"I don't have time!" she said, and ran off to meet Kien-Niou.

So the Sun asked the Herdsman to go back to work, too.

"I'm busy!" he said.

The Sun called all the stars together and gave them the bad news.

"I just can't persuade them," he said. "We're going to have to try something else."

The stars came up with a new idea. If the Weaver Girl and the Herdsman couldn't concentrate on their work when they were together, then they would have to be separated.

First, the Sun went and asked Tchi-Niu to help him mend his socks.

"It's an emergency!" he said. "I have to walk to Pluto tomorrow, and my feet are covered in blisters!"

She sighed and agreed to work at her loom for just a little while. Then, Venus went and asked Kien-Niou to follow her.

"I think one of your cattle is injured!" she said.

The Herdsman didn't want to leave his wife, but he couldn't bear to think of any of his cattle in pain. He followed Venus away from the Moon and deep into the Solar System.

When the lovers were hard at work, the stars dug a deep channel through space and flooded it with light. The channel made a river of starlight, distant suns, planets, and asteroids that meandered through space—cutting a path between Tchi-Niu and Kien-Niou.

At last, Tchi-Niu glanced up from her work and cried out in horror. She was separated from her husband! The wide river of the Milky Way flowed between them, impossible to cross.

The Weaver Girl turned to her father with tears in her eyes.

"What have you done?" she asked, weeping. "How can I see my husband with this river between us?"

The Sun was filled with sadness, but he could not relent.

"I'm sorry, my daughter," he said, "but this was the only way. You and Kien-Niou have been neglecting your work. The stars and the Earth are suffering. It's time for you to go back to your weaving, and for the Herdsman to go back to his cattle."

"How can I survive like this?" sobbed Tchi-Niu. "I love him!"

"What if we made a deal?" the Sun said, kindly. "I need you to stay here and weave. But once a year, I could spare you for a brief visit to the Herdsman, so long as you promise to cross back over before dawn."

"I promise, I promise!" said Tchi-Niu.

The Sun sent word across the river to see if Kien-Niou would agree, too. Both the lovers solemnly swore that they would honor the agreement.

Then the Sun put two fingers to his lips and let out a loud, high-pitched whistle. There was a flurry of wings as a cloud of birds rose up from the Earth: neat black-and-white magpies dressed in their best formal suits.

One of them hopped forward and tipped its head to the Weaver Girl in a deep bow.

"We are here to carry you across the river, my lady," he said. "Please step this way."

As Tchi-Niu watched in amazement, the magpies filed out over the Milky Way, flying wing tip to wing tip. They covered the river of light so thickly that she could walk all the way across, held up by soft feathers, without the slightest stumble or hesitation.

"Just remember—be back by dawn!" the Sun called after her.

And indeed, Tchi-Niu and Kien-Niou kept their word. To this day, they meet once a year across the magpie bridge, on the seventh day of the seventh month.

So if you see a magpie out on his own on that day, you'd better ask him: Don't you have work to do?

THE BURIED MOON

Based on a traditional German story

Once upon a time, in a village not so far away from here, it was always dark at night. You had to light a candle just to see the end of your own nose. Every day at sunset, people would lock their doors, shutter their windows, and close their eyes tight until the morning. The days were so short in the winter that they didn't even have time to cook dinner or wash their clothes.

One crisp December day, four young men gathered around the village well to complain about it.

"I'm sick of only eating sandwiches," said one of them. "I miss hot meals!"

"I haven't read a good book in months," said another, longingly. "I can't get past chapter one before it gets dark."

"Last week, I tripped over my slippers and woke everyone up falling down the stairs," sighed the third.

The fourth young man looked thoughtfully at his friends.

"Well, it's no use complaining," he said. "This has been going on for hundreds of

years, and it's high time we did something about it."

His friends nodded uncertainly.

"But … what could we do?" asked the first young man.

"There are stories," said the second young man. "I've heard tales about a land where it's so bright, people stay up all night. You can ride from dusk till dawn, and your horse won't even falter, the path is so clear."

"But how would we find such a place?"

"We'll set out by night," said the fourth young man, firmly. "We'll carry a lantern to light the path. Before it's lit, we'll look for the brightest place in the sky, and we'll walk in that direction for as long as we can."

The four friends set out the very next night. Each one carried a bundle with a clean shirt (although there hadn't been time to iron it) and a pack of sandwiches (sliced any which way in the dark).

They walked for three nights, sleeping during the day. At first, each one was secretly worried that they had come on a fool's errand. Was there really a whisper of light in that far-distant corner of the dark sky? But as the road rolled away under their feet, the light grew brighter, and they marched along more quickly and cheerfully than before.

On the fourth night, the sky grew so bright that they blew out the lantern. They could see perfectly well without it. The light grew stronger as they followed a wide track with rough stones laid along it, scored with deep grooves from carriage wheels. They knew that there must be people nearby.

At last, they reached the town where the night shone bright as day. The four friends stood in the town

square, struck dumb with amazement. People haggling at market stalls, fetching water at the pump and even tending their gardens by night, while children ran around playing.

The fourth young man gestured to one of the children to come over.

"Excuse me," he said, "can you tell me why the night is so bright here?"

"Oh!" said the little girl. "That's because of our Moon."

The four young men looked at each other. They didn't know what a Moon was, but they were too embarrassed to say so.

"Where might we find him—her—it?" stuttered the second young man.

The girl looked at him scornfully.

"On the east edge of town, of course," she said, "in the moon-tree."

"Of course," agreed the third young man, hastily. "Come on, friends. Let's go to the moon-tree."

But as they walked away, their minds were in consternation. What was a Moon? A kind of machine? An animal from the forest? A kind of fruit?

They were not expecting what they saw on the edge of town. A huge, ancient oak tree, so aged and twisted that its lowest branches swooped against the ground, stood illuminated in a clearing. In its topmost branches, there was a disk of light with craters and scratches on its face. Ropes and hooks held it securely to the tree, some of them worn and ragged, some only recently added. It was the Moon.

The four young men walked toward it in silence. They had never seen such a thing: like a sun made of silver or hundreds of stars crushed together.

"Can I help you?" said a hearty voice behind them.

They turned to see a red-faced man in a red coat, with a ladder under his arm. He had gold lacing on his coat, gold trimming on his hat, and even one gold tooth.

"Please would you tell us about this Moon?" asked one of the young men.

"Ah!" said the shiny, cheerful man—although his smile slipped a little. "That's my Moon. I found it and I trapped it, and now I keep it tethered up in this tree. The townsfolk pay me a penny a day to top it up with oil and polish its face."

Sure enough, they noticed that the moon-keeper was holding a rusty oil can.

"Its face doesn't look very polished," said the first young man, politely. "I think I can see some scratches."

The moon-keeper's eyes darted from side to side.

"I don't have to explain myself to you," he blustered. "It's my Moon! Mine! And I only share it with these people out of the goodness of my heart. It's mine, I tell you."

The four young men looked at each other, a silent conversation passing between them. Then they said farewell to the moon-keeper and walked back into the town.

While they ate a hearty dinner at the inn, they discussed what they had seen.

"I didn't like that old man," said the first young man, bluntly.

"I don't think the Moon even really belongs to him," said the second.

"Imagine how different our lives would be, if we had a Moon like that!" said the third.

The fourth young man looked thoughtful again.

"I think we might be able to do something about that, friends," he said.

They waited until day dawned and all the townsfolk went to bed. They left money on the table to pay for their room and board, but they stole the blankets off their beds, and a horse and cart out of the inn stables. As they trundled the cart quietly out of town, the fourth young man reached over a garden wall and picked up a pair of big hedge shears that someone had left outside.

They went straight to the moon-tree. This time, there was no one about.

"Quick, boys," said the fourth young man, who was certainly the cleverest among them. "I'll climb the tree and cut the Moon free with these shears. You stand below and guide it into the cart. And make sure you cover it with the blankets, so the townsfolk don't notice what we're up to."

So that's what they did. Then they drove home, three days and three nights, with their path lit by the Moon.

When they got back to their own village, they tied the Moon up again. The four friends took turns to oil it and polish its face, although they never quite got all the scratches out. Eventually, people forgot that they had ever been held hostage by the dark of night.

Even the dwarves and the elves crept out of the forest and made friends with the villagers under the moonlight.

But I am sorry to say that as the four friends grew older, they became more and more like the old moon-keeper in that faraway town. They thought that the Moon belonged to them. And when the fourth friend died, he said that his share of the Moon should be buried with him.

His friends lopped off a quarter of the Moon's face with the same rusty hedge shears, and they buried it with their friend's coffin in the churchyard. It seemed to them that the nights grew a little darker, but they thought that was just because they missed their friend. Even the days were dimmer without him.

Time passed, and another of the friends died. He had written his will the same way. They held his funeral, followed by a wake with a delicious hot dinner (and certainly no sandwiches), and another quarter of the Moon was buried.

The next friend followed soon after. When the last friend got sick, he said to his family, "I've missed my friends. It's time for me to go. Just make sure that my share of the Moon is buried with me, too."

That was how the whole Moon got buried. The four men were brave, adventurous, and they were certainly very good friends to each other. But that was their one big mistake.

The nights were completely dark again. Soon, people began to trip over, bump into each other, fall down the stairs, get lost in the woods. The milkmaids on their morning rounds fell over and spilled all the

milk. The dwarves got mixed up and started mining the walls of people's houses instead of the rocks. The elves sneaked into the mayor's garden and ate all the fruit off his fruit trees. The entire village was in chaos.

Now the four friends were in heaven, looking down at their old home in dismay. They realized that they had made a terrible mistake.

St. Peter called them before him to explain themselves.

"We're very sorry," said the fourth friend, hanging his head. "In fact, I'm sorry. It was my fault. I thought the Moon belonged to me."

"Well, it doesn't," said St. Peter in a very stern voice, but with a twinkle in his eye. "I'm afraid this is what happens when people stay up all night and start behaving badly. I'm going to have to go down there and sort it all out."

"We really are sorry," mumbled the other friends. "Can we help?"

"I think you'd better stay here," twinkled St. Peter. "Just don't go after the Sun while I'm away, all right?"

St. Peter locked up the gates of heaven safely behind him with his big ring of keys and whistled for his horse. Then he leaped up into the saddle, for he was still nimble for an old saint, and trotted down through the dark night sky to the village.

The first thing he did was send everybody to sleep. The dwarves returned to their burrows, the elves to their trees, and the village people went quietly to their beds.

The second thing he did was to free the Moon. St. Peter and his horse clip-clopped through the suddenly silent village, tut-tutting at the mess, until they reached the graveyard where the four friends and the Moon were buried.

It did not take Saint Peter long to clear the earth away without disturbing the four friends. He reached out and gently brushed the soil from the Moon's face.

"Poor old Moon," he said. "Look at all the wrinkles you've picked up, just like me! It's high time you were back in the sky where you belong."

The third thing he did was help the Moon up onto the horse, sitting on the saddle behind him. Then St. Peter and the Moon rode up into the sky, where the Moon still shines freely for everyone to see.

Tama-rereti Goes Fishing

Based on Maori myths

This is a story from a long time ago, when the birds were as big as people, the trees were as tall as mountains, and the sky at night was a blank, black slate, with no stories written on it yet.

Tama-rereti was a great hunter in that time. One morning, he woke up feeling hungry. He poked his head outdoors and said,

"Hey! What do we have for breakfast?"

"What did you catch yesterday?" asked his wife. "Unless you're hiding some fish under the bed, there's nothing left!"

(Back then, if you wanted fish for breakfast, you had to go and catch it yourself.)

So Tama-rereti went down to the shore of the great lake where he lived, checked over his canoe, and set off onto the water.

Now I have already told you that Tama-rereti was a great hunter. He was clever with a fishhook, could track any animal by its footprints, and could move as silently as the sun creeping across the grass. But on this particular day, all his skill was for nothing.

There were just no fish. He tried the rocky shallows on the shore of the lake, where the little fish liked to dart in and out: nothing.

He paddled farther out, where the medium-sized fish used to laze around in the cool depths: nothing. He paddled even farther out, where it was too deep to see the bottom of the lake, and the biggest fish of all would swim smoothly in the current: nothing at all.

It was as if he was the only living creature out on the lake that day.

By this time, the sun was high in the sky, and it was getting hot. Tama-rereti began to feel very sleepy.

"I'll just take a short nap," he told himself. "When I wake up, all the fish will have woken up too."

He stowed his paddle away and lay down in the bottom of the canoe. He was asleep within minutes. The sun sparkled on the peaceful waters of the lake, and a gentle breeze

stirred past. Sure enough, after a little while, the fish woke up and began to swim around the canoe as usual—but Tama-rereti slept on.

Have you ever told yourself that you were going to have a quick rest, but then slept for hours and hours? Have you ever laid down for a nap in the afternoon and woken up in the dark? That's what happened to Tama-rereti.

By the time he woke up, the sun had disappeared between the hills, and the night was pitch-dark. The only sound he could hear was the waves lapping around the canoe.

"Hello!" he called out. But his voice echoed away into the darkness. Tama-rereti had drifted all the way out into the middle of the great lake. He could only just make out the shadow of the shore in the distance.

Now Tama-rereti began to get a little nervous. He was a big, brave man, but it was very dark out on that lake. And he knew that it was on dark nights like this one that the taniwha would come out of their hiding places and look for something to eat.

The taniwha were the creatures that lived in dark caves and deep pools; the spirits that coiled through the currents and rippled their bodies along the waves. They had keen, keen eyes and sharp, sharp teeth, and they were always hungry.

Meanwhile, Tama-rereti was alone in the darkness, a very long way from home.

He took a deep breath, and even the sound of his breath seemed to echo across the cool, still lake. Then he sat up, lit a torch to hang on the prow of the canoe, and picked up his paddle.

"I'll never get home if I just sit here waiting for the taniwha to find me," he said. "I'd better start paddling."

Slowly and quietly, he dipped his paddle in the water and began to move the canoe along. He didn't know which way to go, because there was no land in sight, and the sky was an empty sheet of darkness. He just faced the prow of the boat and kept paddling.

He paddled that canoe for a long time. It seemed like hours before he noticed that the water felt different under his paddle. The little waves of the lake had smoothed out, and he could feel a long, lazy current carrying him forward.

He could even see fish. Some big kokopu fish, spangled with gold and silver, were

swimming alongside the canoe as he went. Their glittering skin shed light onto the water and glimmered on the white pebbles on the floor of the lake.

Tama-rereti could feel that the water was flowing faster and faster. The canoe raced forward with the fish dashing along beside it. He began to feel the strangest sensation, as if the canoe was leaning upward as well as forward.

Now you can see what happened here. Paddling away in the darkness, not knowing where he was going, Tama-rereti had accidentally drifted into the river that carries the water up into the sky to make it rain. His canoe was carried straight up into the heavens from the great lake. But he didn't know that—at least, not to begin with.

On he sailed, through the vast dark ocean of space. Planets floated past like glowing jellyfish; asteroids darted by his canoe like hundreds of tiny, gleaming fish. From time to time, a black hole spun in the distance like a whirlpool. Tama-rereti watched the sky in wonder. But he didn't feel scared anymore, because he could still see the kokopu swimming steadily along beside him, their scales reflecting off the pebbles on the riverbed.

Then he had an idea. Beyond the river, the sky was dark; there was no way home for him to follow. But the river stones shone brightly.

Tama-rereti leaned over the side of his boat and scooped his hand into the riverbed. The pebbles ran between his fingers like silver and pearls. Then he stood up, clutching a few stones in his hand, and threw them up into the sky.

The pebbles stayed where he had thrown them, making a pattern across the sky and shedding light across the course of the river. Tama-rereti realized that they were pointing the way home. He picked up his paddle again and began to row with more energy than before. Whenever he ran out of light, he threw another handful of pebbles into the sky. The fish raced alongside him, trying to keep up!

He continued in this way for some time. He had drifted a long way from home, so he still had a long way to go. Then, after a while, he noticed a shadow ahead of him in the river: a tall shape with a bobble on top. Sometimes he thought it was moving, and sometimes it seemed to stay still.

"Maybe it's a taniwha," Tama-rereti thought. "I'll have to be really careful now.

Almost home! Just a little bit farther!"

He slowed down and tried to paddle silently, but the waters still rippled around him. He drew closer and closer to the mysterious, shadowy figure until he could almost reach out and touch it.

Then the figure turned around. Tama-rereti nearly fell off his canoe.

The figure laughed.

"Tama-rereti, my brave hunter," he said, "did you think I was a taniwha? It's me, Ranginui!"

Ranginui was the god of the sky. Tama-rereti knew that he wasn't a monster, but he was worried about what Ranginui would think of all the river pebbles.

"I'm sorry if—" he stuttered. "I mean, I didn't—I was just trying to—"

"You were just trying to get home, I know," said Ranginui. "And truth be told, I love the stars you've made! Now my sky looks more magnificent than ever. All the people back on Earth will look up at it, instead of staring at their feet."

Then he hopped into the canoe beside Tama-rereti and grabbed the second paddle.

"Quickly now, Tama-rereti!" said the sky god. "Let's get you home before dawn!"

Sure enough, with the god's help, the canoe went faster than ever, and they were soon back at the shore of the great lake. Ranginui reached into the water and scooped up one of the great kokopu fish that had followed them through the sky.

"Take this to your family for breakfast," he said, "and they won't mind that you were missing all night. Goodbye, Tama-rereti! I'll be keeping an eye on your adventures!"

Tama-rereti never saw Ranginui again. But people did say that he had the best luck at hunting and fishing. He always came home with big, gleaming fish that shone just like the stars, and he never got lost at night. He taught all his family how to navigate by the pebbles that shone in the sky as a river of stars.

He lived a long, happy life on Earth—but he never forgot to look upward. And when Tama-rereti was old, and it was time for him to die, Ranginui carried his canoe up into the heavens. You can still see Te Waka O Tama-rereti shining up there in the southern sky, if you know where to look.

SOL and SKOLL

Based on Norse myths

If you wake up early enough one morning, you will see Sol coming over the horizon. There, against the cold, gloomy sky, you'll see her flame-red hair and her bright smile. As she climbs higher in the sky with her gleaming chariot and her fiery horses, she brings light across the land, painting the world with warmth and life. If you wave at her, you'll feel her smile suddenly beam your way.

Back in the days of the Vikings, everybody knew who Sol was. When people tumbled blearily out of bed to milk the cows, knead the bread, and launch the fishing boats, they'd watch for Sol's light.

But although the people loved Sol, I'm afraid to say that there were some creatures who didn't like her. The frost giants, skulking in the mountains, would cringe and cower when they heard the rumble of her chariot overhead. The old gods, plotting revenge from the edge of the world, would scowl and spit when her light touched their heads. They missed the days when the world was cold, icy, and dark.

Those nasty old monsters got together and made a plan to get rid of Sol. They

didn't want the Earth to be warm. They didn't want people to enjoy the sunshine. They didn't like crops growing, animals playing, and people exploring the world. They wanted it to be still, dark, empty night, all the time.

"We should chase her out of the sky!" growled one of the frost giants.

"We should scatter her horses and shatter her chariot!" snarled a mean old god.

"It's time the sky belonged to us again!" agreed another.

They went searching through the deep woods, where Sol's light couldn't quite reach, for the biggest and scariest wolf they could find. They called him Skoll.

Skoll was the size of a horse, with teeth like knives. His eyes gleamed in the darkness, his fur was tipped with shards of ice, and he could run faster than any human.

The giants lifted Skoll up into the sky and showed him where Sol's chariot was just rising over the horizon.

"Get her! Get her!" they howled. Skoll took off with one giant leap and began to chase after the sun goddess's swift chariot, with his teeth bared and his tongue slavering out of his mouth.

Sol heard Skoll growling and turned back to look. In an instant, she realized what had happened: the wolf, covered in ice and snow, must belong to the frost giants and old gods who hated the sun. She whipped up her horses and set off across the sky faster than ever.

At first, she kept ahead of Skoll easily. She wheeled and weaved, ducked and dived, and the wolf never came close. But as the day wore on, her horses, Arvakr and Alsvidr, began to get tired. The great bellows at the front of her chariot, which blew

ceaselessly on the horses to keep them cool, began to puff ineffectually. Her pace slowed, and her light grew dimmer.

Skoll kept running. It seemed he would never wear out. He crept closer and closer to the wheels of Sol's chariot, snarling and snapping at her heels. She felt his hot breath on the back of her neck and the chilly drops of ice shaken from his fur. Her bright sunlight began to waver uncertainly, and the wolf's ice made a halo of mist around her chariot.

Back on Earth, people watched in horror as they saw the sun turn cloudy and start to flicker. It had been a sunny morning, but suddenly the shadows began to lengthen and the sky turned dark.

"It's the end of the world!" someone cried out. "The frost giants are back!"

"The old gods are taking their revenge!"

"Darkness is coming! Darkness is coming!"

They could hear the rattle of Sol's chariot and the thundering of Arvakr and Alsvidr's hooves—and always, behind them, the steady thud of Skoll's paws and the terrible growling in the back of his throat. Sol went faster and faster, but it seemed that Skoll would be faster still.

By now, everyone had come out of their houses to watch. Farmers paused in the fields, and fishers dropped their nets as they stared up into the sky. It felt as if there was nothing they could do. The world was going to end, and nobody could do anything about it.

Sol was feeling hopeless, too. Her beautiful, strong horses were panting and sweating with the effort of pulling the chariot along. She could feel her light growing dim even as she tried to shine brighter and drive faster. She could hear the distant, crackly laughter of the frost giants as they watched from their mountain fortresses. As far as she looked across the sky, she couldn't see help coming from anywhere.

But help was coming.

In one tiny village, nestled between the hills and the sea, as if an eagle had dropped it out of the sky, a woman named Dagny was staring up at the sun. She could see that Sol was in trouble. The icy mist and the growing darkness around Skoll made it hard to see, but she could hear the horrible snarling and growling that he made.

"Astrid! Come here a minute," she called out to her friend. "Can you hear that?"

"It sounds like a wolf," said Astrid.

"That's right," agreed Dagny. "And I don't know much about frost monsters … but I do know that wolves hate loud noises."

The two friends looked at each other for a second. Then they both turned around and ran back inside their houses.

Dagny headed straight for the fireplace where the cooking pots were stacked up and ready to use. She grabbed a long wooden spoon and the biggest, roundest pot. Then she dashed back outside and began to drum the spoon against the pot. *Clang, bang, crash, bash!*

Astrid was already running down the street, banging her pot and shouting to the other people who were standing and watching the sky.

"Quick! Quick! Bring your pots! Bring your pans!"

"We have to scare the wolf away!" Dagny called. "It's the only way we can help Sol!"

At first, no one listened. They were all transfixed by the chase that was happening far above them, as Skoll slunk closer and closer to Sol's chariot.

But then they began to notice the noise. One by one, people turned and ran into their houses. They came back out with everything they could find to make a noise: pots, pans, spoons, fire irons, forks, drinking horns, and even swords and shields! Blacksmiths hammered at their anvils, and musicians blew on their horns and pipes. They rattled and banged and clattered and yelled until you couldn't even hear yourself think. *Bash, clang, bang, bing, boom!*

"Go away, Skoll!" screamed Astrid. "Leave our sun alone!"

"You can do it, Sol!" Dagny shouted. "Don't give up now! We're all on your side!"

High in the sky above the little village, Sol could only dimly hear the noise. She was totally focused on steering her chariot and urging the horses on through the darkness. The reins were slick in her hands, and sweat dripped into her eyes.

Everything started to feel wobbly and distant. Sol's eyes were closing, the sound faded in her ears, and her knees trembled as she slumped forward in a dead faint.

Arvakr and Alsvidr felt her hands drop from the reins. They tossed their heads in

fright as they saw the sky grow darker still. Skoll hadn't caught the sun goddess yet—but her light was going out. The two horses surged forward, trying to escape Skoll on their own, but knowing that it was hopeless without Sol to guide them.

But then something strange happened.

Arvakr and Alsvidr had felt the wolf's hot breath on their hind legs and heard his teeth snap at their feet. They knew that he was pelting along behind them. But as they tried to pull Sol to safety, they realized that Skoll had dropped behind.

Dagny and Astrid were watching from the ground when Skoll whined and pulled back. As the clanging and banging sound grew overwhelming, he stopped running and rolled over onto his back. He thrashed and wriggled with his paws over his ears. He hated the loud noises.

The women could see Sol's chariot pulling ahead as the wolf squirmed in the sky. He began to howl—a horrible, shrill noise—to drown out the clatter from below.

Meanwhile, Sol was coming back to her senses. She began to stir and open her eyes. The two flame-tipped horses were still running as fast as they could, but Alsvidr looked back over his shoulder to whicker softly to her.

Sol groaned and put a hand to her head. Then she reached for the reins and slowly pulled herself up on the side of the chariot.

She couldn't believe her eyes. The awful wolf Skoll was lying helplessly behind them. As Sol woke, her light slowly began to dawn across the world again, illuminating the village below. The people's faces shone with fierce joy. Their cooking pans and shields glittered in the sunlight.

Sol leaned over the chariot and waved to them.

"Thank you!" she called out. "I will never forget your help today!"

Astrid blushed fiery red. Dagny waved back. Then all the people of the Viking village let out a huge cheer as Sol's horses burst forward again, sweeping their path across the sky.

But what about Skoll? And what about the frost giants and the old gods who set him on the sun?

When the noise stopped, Skoll crept back to his dark, quiet woods, and it was a long time before he came out again. He had never heard such a horrible noise as all those people shouting and drumming before. The frost giants were furious, and the old gods swore that they would get revenge, but there was nothing they could do. They had to admit that they had failed. They grumbled and chittered where Sol's sunlight fell on them; they scowled and hid in the shadows.

Many, many, many months later, there came a day when they persuaded Skoll out of his lair. They sent him out across the sky after Sol again.

But the Vikings were always ready again, with their cauldrons, goblets, pots, pans, swords, shields, drums, and trumpets.

The wolf has never caught Sol yet. Every morning, you can see her ride out in her chariot with Arvakr and Alsvidr. You'll see her light sweep across the land as she follows the same path across the sky.

One day, you might even see Skoll running behind her. If you see ice shimmering around the sun, or it suddenly grows dark in the middle of the day, then you'll know that the wolf is nipping at Sol's heels.

And if you see that happen, what will you do?

Well, if you're a true Viking, you'll grab whatever you can find—pots and pans, drums, instruments, tools—and make enough noise to scare the wolf away. Skoll will slink back to his dark mountain forests, and Sol will wave her thanks to you.

The Feathered Serpent and the Moon Rabbit

Based on an Aztec tale

Have you ever heard of Quetzalcoatl? In the vast empire of the Aztecs, he was the wisest, craftiest, and strongest of them all. And oh! He was beautiful.

Quetzalcoatl strode across the hills and plains with a conch shell gleaming on his chest. His shoulders shone with a cape of shimmering quetzal feathers. Rattlesnakes hissed and curled around his waist. Where he walked, the trees trembled, and the sun shone brighter. When he ran, he was faster than the wind and the light. They called him the Feathered Serpent and the Wisest One.

But there was a problem with being the Wisest One. Quetzalcoatl got bored.

He had already journeyed across the continent to find maize and chocolate and bring them back to people. He had already written the first book and marked the first calendar. He had even soared through the sky as the Morning Star. Now he felt like there was nothing left to do.

So, one morning, Quetzalcoatl got up early and swung on his cape of eagle and quetzal feathers. He coiled his belt of snakes tightly around his waist and hung the gleaming conch shell around his neck. Then he started walking.

He decided that he was going to walk west until he reached the sea, and then he would start swimming. Surely something exciting would happen to him then.

Quetzalcoatl set off through the Valley of Mexico, across the wide plateau and past the chinampa islands covered with young maize. The fields ruffled with wind as he passed them. People stopped and stared when he went by—the rattling snakes at his belt and the gleaming feathers on his cape were unmistakable.

But Quetzalcoatl didn't stop to talk to the people, not this time. He kept on heading west.

He walked day and night, without stopping to rest, eat, or drink. He walked until the feathers around his shoulders were threadbare and shabby. The shiny conch shell around his neck was covered with dust. One by one, his rattlesnakes slid away into the undergrowth to search for food without him. Quetzalcoatl was finally alone in the wilderness.

He began to feel tired and weak. That was something new, but it didn't feel very exciting. His feet hurt, his mouth was dry, and his skin sweated and itched under the heavy cape of feathers.

Still, he kept walking. The Feathered Serpent had lost his feathers and his serpents. The Wisest One did not seem very wise anymore. He just kept moving. All he could think about was putting one foot in front of the other.

Perhaps you have felt like this on a very long walk or on a busy day when you don't have time to eat. Even the smartest person will start to feel a bit stupid when they are hungry, thirsty, and tired. Quetzalcoatl forgot all about his mission to find something exciting. Instead, he just thought about walking on and on and on.

He continued on like this for days or maybe even weeks. (Feathered Serpents are better at surviving hunger than normal people are.) But eventually—even through the fog of thirst and exhaustion—he realized that he was in big trouble. Quetzalcoatl had lost all of his strength.

He sat down on the ground in the middle of the forest. He couldn't see where he had started from, and he couldn't see the ocean. He was hopelessly lost. When he tried to get up again, he discovered that he was too weak to stand on his own.

Lying in the dust, he turned his head to look around him. There was no water in sight; no plants to eat. Quetzalcoatl realized that he had made a terrible mistake. A single tear trickled down his cheek and onto the ground.

He could hear a steady, regular thumping sound. He thought it must be his heart beating out its final beats, alone in the forest. *Thump-thump, thump-thump, thump-thump.*

But Quetzalcoatl was wrong again. The thumping sound wasn't his heartbeat. It was a young jackrabbit who had hopped over to see what was going on.

She crouched down beside Quetzalcoatl and rubbed her velvety nose against his, her whiskers quivering. He could see the late afternoon sunshine glowing through her elegant long ears.

"Are you thirsty?" she asked.

"Yes," croaked Quetzalcoatl.

"There's no food nearby," she said. "I'm only passing through myself. But you could eat me, if you like. I'm not very important."

Quetzalcoatl was astonished. Without any hesitation, and without knowing who he was, the jackrabbit had selflessly offered up her life for his.

"I can't let you do that," he said, humbly. "And you seem very important to me."

"But you're dying of thirst," said the jackrabbit.

"That's true," said Quetzalcoatl the Wise One, and he lay and thought for a moment. Then he said, "I have another idea."

He took off the conch shell from around his neck and hung it on the jackrabbit. Then he asked her to hop as fast as she could to the nearest river and fill it with water for him.

The jackrabbit was happy to oblige, but Quetzalcoatl was very thirsty, and the conch shell only held a little water. She had to make many journeys.

Once Quetzalcoatl had drunk his fill, he tried to stand up. But his legs trembled; he swayed back and forth and fell back onto the ground.

"What's wrong now?" asked the jackrabbit, anxiously.

"I'm hungry," said Quetzalcoatl. "I haven't eaten since I started my journey."

"I think I saw some berries growing near the river," the jackrabbit said. She picked up the conch shell again and hopped away to forage for food. But the conch shell could only hold a few fruits at a time, so once again, she had to make many trips before the Feathered Serpent was satisfied.

By the time Quetzalcoatl was strong enough to stand again, it was late at night. The sky had grown dark, and the Moon sailed above them like a great silver coin.

"How can I ever thank you enough?" asked Quetzalcoatl, as they stood side by side, watching the night sky.

"I've always wanted to have an adventure," said the jackrabbit wistfully. "That's where I was headed when I saw you. I want to go somewhere that nobody else has ever been."

"I have another idea," said Quetzalcoatl. He was starting to feel much more like the Wisest One by now.

He picked up the jackrabbit gently, being careful not to hurt her long legs or her delicate ears. Then he raised her arms and lifted her high into the sky.

The jackrabbit had never jumped so high. She wondered at the cool air rushing through her fur and blowing her ears back. She kicked her back legs in joy, ready to take off.

"Steady," called out Quetzalcoatl. "Just … a little bit … higher …"

By now the jackrabbit could see stars glittering around her. The planets floated by as if carried by their own invisible current. The Moon came into view like an island appearing over the horizon.

"Now!" said the Feathered Serpent. "Your biggest leap!"

The jackrabbit gathered all her strength and pushed off with her strong back legs, leaping as high as she could toward the Moon.

She landed on the Moon's surface with a soft puff of dust. Although it had looked smooth and silver from the Earth, she was surprised to find that it was covered in rocks and rubble. Colossal dry seas were carved out of its face. As she hopped and snuffled about, she could hear delicate, bell-like music in the air from Quetzalcoatl's sister, the ruler of the Moon, Coyolxauhqui.

But the jackrabbit's most wonderful discovery was the gravity on the Moon. She could bounce six times higher than she could on Earth. The slightest kick of her heels would send her flying above the lunar surface. She sailed across craters and soared up mountainsides. She hopped and ran and corkscrewed with delight.

At last, she saw Quetzalcoatl waving at her from Earth, and she knew it was time to go home. She hopped, skipped, and jumped to the top of the very tallest mountain on the Moon. Then she gathered all her power into her back legs one more time and stepped off into space.

The jackrabbit allowed herself to fall like a diver sinking into deep water, watching the planets and stars flash past her. She hadn't known that there could be anything as big as space: bigger than the land, bigger than the sea, bigger than the blue sky!

She saw the haze of the Earth's atmosphere and felt the cool embrace of the clouds. She saw the outline of the Aztec Empire, a tiny channel between two even more vast continents, surrounded by blue ocean on every side. And she saw Quetzalcoatl, with his arms outstretched to catch her.

The Wisest One, with his power over the wind, made sure that she landed safely. The breeze floated the jackrabbit gently back down to where Quetzalcoatl waited.

"Did you have fun?" he asked.

"It was incredible!" said the jackrabbit. "That was a real adventure!"

"It was the least I could do," said the Feathered Serpent. "You know, when I set out walking, it was because I thought there was nothing interesting left in the world. But you showed me that there's always more to see."

The two of them stood looking up at the Moon for a while.

"I'll never forget today," the jackrabbit said softly.

"Neither will I," said Quetzalcoatl. "In fact … I think I have another idea."

He reached up with both hands toward the Moon and began to trace lines on its surface. His fingers left long shadows in the dust, visible all the way from Earth.

First, he drew a long, upright shape. Then he drew front legs and back legs. Last of all, he drew two long ears. It was a jackrabbit!

"There you go," he said. "Now this day will never be forgotten. People will remember you every time they look up at the Moon." And it was quite true. When Quetzalcoatl was well enough to continue his journey, he walked all across the Aztec lands, telling everyone how the jackrabbit had helped him.

If you look into the night sky on a full moon, you can still see Quetzalcoatl's drawing of the rabbit. And, if you're ever lucky enough to see a jackrabbit at night, you will see it hopping, skipping, and jumping as high as it can—trying to leap as high as the Moon.

The Little Girl with a Big Voice

Based on South African stories

Once upon a time, there was a young girl who lived in the veld, the wide, flat grassland of South Africa. She was not very tall or very strong, but she had a big voice.

She had a big voice from the very day she was born. When she fussed in her crib, the ground would shake. When she shouted, all the birds would rise up out of the trees, chattering and fluttering. And whenever she cried, the heavens would open and cover the land with rain.

On the day that our story begins, she was feeling very sad. She had just woken up feeling like something was wrong. It was the kind of day where the weather can't make up its mind and nothing goes right.

The little girl sat down outside her house and started to cry. She decided she was going to have a really good cry—the kind that makes you thirsty afterward—and let all her feelings out.

But this was bad news for everybody else in the village. The second she sat down outside her house, the air trembled with thunder, and the wind blew a little colder. As the

first tear trickled down the little girl's cheek, the villagers felt the first faint misty drops of rain. And by the time she opened her mouth and began to cry in earnest, it was pouring sheets of water from the sky.

She cried, and cried, and cried. Dogs whimpered and ran indoors. Clothes sagged on washing lines. Birds were rained out of the sky until they had to run around on land with their tiny feet splashing through the puddles. Farmers working the fields watched in alarm as their tools floated away and their plants began to drown.

Sometimes it feels good to cry just as hard as you can. But the little girl didn't get to enjoy her cry for very long.

There was a grumpy woman who lived next door to the little girl. All the children in the village were scared of her. She used to complain about noise and laundry and smoke from cooking fires and which vegetables people should plant and where children were allowed to play and …

Well, in short, just about anything that happened, she was ready to be cross about. On this occasion, she was cross about the little girl crying.

The grumpy woman popped out of her house and went straight up to the little girl.

"Can't you hush that noise?" she said, angrily. "Nobody wants to hear you complaining! And look at the mess you've made! Everything is going wrong!"

"I'm *crying!*" said the little girl, with dignity (even though her cheeks were wet with tears).

"Do you think I care about that?" said the woman, working herself up into a frenzy. "Get out of here! Take your crying somewhere else!"

The little girl stuck her tongue out at the grumpy woman and ran off. As she ran through the village, she felt very hard done by. She was already having a bad day. Couldn't people let her be miserable in peace?

There was only one solution, she decided. She was going to run away. She would go out onto the veld and live her own life—free to cry as much as she wanted, whenever she wanted.

So when she reached the edge of the village, she kept on walking, past the well, past the fields, to where the sky arced over the endless landscape. The breeze sighed softly in the grass, and antelope grazed peacefully in the distance.

Soon she didn't feel like crying anymore. There was too much to explore. She lay on her back in the grass and watched the birds swooping overhead until it felt like her whole head was full of blue sky. She felt warm and peaceful.

She stayed there for hours while the blue sky slowly changed to twilight and the air began to cool. The grass whispered secrets to her and the birds called out their good nights. Finally, she decided, it was time to go home.

But there were more animals on the veld—animals that were not so friendly.

The little girl scrambled to her feet and looked around for the path back to the village. She could see the trail that had brought her there, but this time, the way was blocked. Six pairs of glittering eyes stared back at her from the gloom.

It was a pride of lions!

She stared back at them bravely. They didn't even blink.

She took a step toward them. Her footstep sounded as loud as a drum. But when the three lions padded toward her, too, their feet didn't make a sound.

Her heart sank. She had stayed out too late, and now these lions were going to eat her up. One of them was already licking its lips.

The more she thought about it, the more unfair it felt. She'd had a bad day. That grumpy woman had shouted at her. She'd run away from home, and nobody had even come to look for her. And now these lions were going to eat her?

The little girl had had enough. She stood up straight and glared at the lions.

She stared for so long that her eyes started to water. At first, there didn't seem to be any effect, but then one of the lions blinked.

She glared at them even harder. She was furious. She bundled up all her anger and beamed it out of her eyes at them.

One of the lions whimpered. Another one pawed the ground nervously.

But the little girl glared and glared and glared and GLARED.

That pride of lions just couldn't take it anymore. They'd thought they were going to get a nice, quick snack—but instead, they were getting stared at by a little girl who looked very cross. They glanced at each other uneasily.

They weren't sure what to do, so they did what any lion would do in a tight corner. They decided to hurry up and eat her.

The lions lunged forward with a great roar, their teeth bared. But the little girl didn't even flinch. She just kept glaring.

By now, the lions were dashing toward her at full speed. Her gaze never wavered. Blue sparks began to appear around the lions' paws. Red flames crackled along their backs and flickered between their teeth.

The little girl kept staring. The lions were almost at her throat.

And then …

And then …

BOOM!

The lions exploded into bursts of brilliant blue and white light. Their bodies disappeared and left bright, burning spheres that spread out in all directions. Then those balls of fire took off into the night sky, past the clouds, past the moon, until they were just distant stars glimmering against the darkness.

Finally, the little girl blinked. Then she took a deep breath. She was suddenly feeling tired. You see, she'd stared at the lions so hard and had been so angry, that she had exploded them into stars. And that takes a lot of energy.

She set off down the trail that led back to the village. She had let out all her anger, and now she was ready for some dinner.

By the time she got home, it was pitch-black (except for the patch of sky where the lions glittered as constellations) and very cold. The little girl was very hungry indeed. She could see the cooking fires outside the houses as she trudged along. There was a delicious smell of roasting roots in the air.

Now as it happened, the first house that she came to was where the grumpy woman lived. The little girl knew that anybody in the village would share their dinner with someone who was hungry, so she went up to the woman and said:

"Please may I have something to eat? I've been gone all day!" Then she added, "And I'm not crying anymore. I'm sorry about this morning."

The grumpy woman put her hands on her hips and looked the little girl up and down.

"You? I'm not sharing my dinner with you!"

"Why not?" asked the little girl, who was trying to be polite.

"I don't want you anywhere near my house! Let me tell you something. I was out gathering firewood at sunset, and I saw what you did to those lions. You're a dangerous kind of person."

"I'm not!" said the little girl. "I just glared at them because they were trying to eat me! I would never hurt anybody."

"You can tell that to the lions," retorted the grumpy woman. "I don't want to hear it! First you flood the village. You ruin my laundry, and you fill my house with chickens. Then you kill the lions. What are you going to do next? Set the sky on fire?"

The little girl took another deep breath. She was tired and hungry, her feet hurt, and nobody had been nice to her all day.

"You know what, you grumpy old woman?" she shouted. "Maybe I will!"

She ran right up to the cooking fire. The woman didn't try to stop her—instead, she jumped back in fear. She really was scared of the little girl who was so tough.

The little girl plunged her hand into the ashes of the fire. She grabbed a fistful of the ashes and the roots that were roasting there. They glowed red and white with heat.

Then she drew back her arm and flung the burning ashes as high as she could into the sky. And she shouted: "I'M—HAVING—A—BAD—DAY!"

The red and white ashes went all the way up into the sky and stuck there, like jewels laid out on a black cloth. They burned and shimmered in a long trail that went from the village to the deepest depths of space. It looked beautiful.

"Look what you've done!" shrieked the grumpy woman. "Everybody, come and see what this child has done! She's made the sky all messy! She's cluttering it up! Come and look at what this naughty girl has done!"

All the other villagers came out of their houses to see what the fuss was about. At first, they were expecting to see something awful. The grumpy woman sounded so very angry.

But then they saw the sky. They stopped right where they were and gazed up at the glorious new trail of stars that the little girl had made—the Milky Way.

"I don't think that looks like a mess," said one of them. "I think it's lovely."

"That's not clutter!" said another. "Those are new stars! What a strong little girl you must be."

The grumpy woman stood with her mouth open as everybody gathered around, congratulating the little girl and asking her what she had been up to all day. They were all delighted with the starry new sky.

"You can't be serious," raged the woman. "This little girl has caused chaos! She's a disaster! She's just *too much!*"

But when she saw that nobody else agreed with her, she went back into her house and slammed the door.

The little girl did get her dinner in the end, after she had told everyone the story of her adventures. And although she still had a big voice and a big temper, she never had quite such a bad day again.

AGLAONIKE CATCHES the MOON

Based on Greek myths

A long, long time ago, Greece was full of witches. There were sea witches who lived in caves and teased sailors with bad storms. There were island witches who raised pigs and grew flowers. There were mountain witches who would make trees move to confuse villagers. There were wind witches who could ride the breeze to the North Pole to go and see the polar bears. There were river witches who could make waterfalls flow backward and fish dance. And there was Aglaonike.

Aglaonike lived in Thessaly, where there were lots of witches, and she was one of the strongest, smartest, and most beautiful of them all. She was very boastful, too, as witches tend to be.

Witches are some of the biggest boasters you'll ever meet. They love to sit around and talk about how smart they are compared to everyone else. The one thing you have to remember, of course, is that they don't always tell the truth.

Witches love hearing each other's boastful stories, and they don't mind whether they're true or not. The trouble only starts when one of them tries to prove her boasts.

One day, all the witches in Thessaly were sitting around bragging to each other about their most successful tricks.

"I can make waves rise higher than a house!" said a sea witch with long green hair and silver fish scales on her feet.

"I can move a mountain a hundred miles!" said a mountain witch with a string of rocky diamonds around her neck.

"Last week, I whipped up a hurricane that tied trees into knots," said a wind witch, wrapping her cloak of eagle feathers around her.

"That's nothing," said an island witch, who had shells braided into her long, curly hair. "I covered an island in so many flowers that you can smell their scent from five miles away."

"Oh, really?" said a river witch, whose brown eyes gleamed and glittered like stones in a stream. "Well, last month, I made a river carve precious stones out of the ground for me. Look at these!" And she let a shimmering handful of gems run through her fingers.

Aglaonike sighed and yawned.

"Are we boring you, Aglaonike?" asked the sea witch.

"Oh, no," said Aglaonike. "But all your ideas seem so small."

"Small?" cried all the witches at once.

"Yes, small! You've got no imagination. I like to think bigger. I'm much, much stronger than water or flowers or hurricanes."

"Prove it!" shouted one of the witches.

"That's easy," said Aglaonike. "I'm so strong that I can move the Moon."

"What utter nonsense," said the mountain witch, who was known for being very sensible and matter-of-fact.

"No one can do that," gasped the wind witch. "It's impossible!"

"Nothing is impossible to me," said Aglaonike proudly. "Before the month is out, I'll bring the Moon to you all in chains!"

Aglaonike was determined to prove that her boasting was true. She left the other witches sitting around gossiping and went back to her workshop to make a plan.

For the next few days, she was so busy that the other witches hardly saw her. Mysterious bangings and clatterings were heard from her workshop, but Aglaonike herself never stopped to talk.

The island witch said that she'd seen Aglaonike picking white daisies; but nobody else had seen her. A fire witch came in from out of town with a cart full of white candles, but when the witches went to buy from her, Aglaonike had already bought them all.

Whatever the great witch was doing, it kept her busy in her workshop every day and every night, until at last it was the time of the full moon.

Witches love the full moon. On a full moon night, they all go outside and picnic under its cool, silvery light. Every single witch was sitting outside, chatting and drinking wine, when Aglaonike finally emerged from her magical workshop.

She was dragging a heavy rope made out of white quartz. As she walked farther away from her house, the rope kept going—it must have been miles long. Finally, she stopped walking and looped the rope around her arm. She lifted the quartz effortlessly and circled it around her head, like a lasso. Then, with a bright chiming sound, she let it go. It looped quickly out toward the Moon … and caught it!

Aglaonike tied the rope to a rock and hurried back inside her house. She came back with an armful of pure white candles. She laid them on the ground in a grid shape and lit them to make an enormous net of white light. Then, with a quick movement of her hands, she picked up the net of lights and flung it over the Moon.

The witches were still and silent with astonishment.

Aglaonike went back inside her house once more and returned with a long string of daisies. She fastened one end of the daisy chain around the Moon and began to pull on the other end.

She tugged and heaved with all her strength. At first, it seemed like nothing was

happening. But then the river witch cried out, "The Moon is getting bigger!"

Sure enough, the Moon was looming larger and larger as Aglaonike pulled it down to Earth. Its light grew stronger until it glowed as clear as day.

"Stop, Aglaonike, stop!" begged the sea witch. "We all believe you now, but please stop! If the Moon is this close, the sea tides will change!"

"Be careful, Aglaonike, please!" chimed in the mountain witch. "It's already bumping against the mountaintops! You'll cause an earthquake if you don't let the Moon go."

But Aglaonike didn't listen. Aglaonike never listened to anybody.

The witches' full moon meeting was very uncomfortable that day. Instead of being bathed in cool, shimmering light, the witches felt too hot. The Moon shone with a glare that hurt their eyes and gave them headaches. They all decided to go home to bed—but nobody could sleep. The Moon glowed so strongly that they could still see its light when they closed their eyes.

When they got up the next day, the witches were tired and cross. But their grumpiness turned to astonishment when they found Aglaonike sitting exactly where they had left her. She had the ropes of quartz, candles, and daisies wrapped around her wrists as the Moon struggled insistently, trying to escape. She looked exhausted.

"Have you been here all night?" gasped the wind witch.

"This stupid Moon keeps trying to wriggle free," said Aglaonike. "But I'm stronger!"

The others shook their heads. Even for a witch, Aglaonike was dangerously proud.

That day was miserable for everyone. The Sun and the Moon kept bumping into each other. Their combined light and heat made the weather far too hot. The island witch sat grieving for the flowers that had withered, and the river witch worried that her streams were going to dry up. But nobody could persuade Aglaonike to move.

At last, the sun set, and the air began to cool a little. The Moon glowed brightly in its bonds. Aglaonike sat in the same place, gripping the ropes tighter than ever.

Then—just as the witches were trying to sleep—someone new came into town.

Nobody was sure exactly where she came from. The sea witch swore that she saw her coming down a staircase of stars; but where the staircase had begun, nobody could say.

She was very beautiful, even compared to the witches (who were each more stunning than the next). Her eyes shone, gems glittered in her hair, and her tunic was made of the purest white wool.

"Aglaonike!" the stranger called out. "Where is Aglaonike?"

"I'm over here," said the great witch, irritably. "I'm too busy to run around after people. You'll have to come to me."

The stranger walked calmly down the road toward Aglaonike. Later, the mountain witch would swear that her feet didn't touch the ground; but nobody could be sure.

"My name is Selene," the stranger said, "and you have stolen something that belongs to me."

The other witches gasped and cowered. Selene was the goddess of the Moon. It had never occurred to them that she would come to fetch the Moon herself.

"It doesn't belong to you anymore," snapped Aglaonike. "I caught the Moon. I'm stronger than you. And now I get to keep it."

"Oh, really?" said Selene. "Well, if you're so strong, I'm sure you won't object to a contest. Whoever wins gets to keep the Moon forever."

"Too easy!" said Aglaonike. "That's not enough of a prize."

"All right, then," said Selene, and she smiled a glimmering smile. "Let's say that whoever wins, gets to keep the Moon … and the other's magic."

The other witches gasped. But Aglaonike laughed harshly.

"Now that's a contest!" she said. "Agreed. How do you want me to prove my magical powers?"

"I see that you have done your finest work already," said Selene, looking at the ropes in the witch's hand. "You spent all week making those chains, didn't you? So, let's make it really easy. You had a week—now I will make a stronger rope, a brighter light, and a prettier flower this very night."

"All in one night?" said the island witch. "That's impossible!"

"I believe Selene can do it," said the mountain witch.

"But Aglaonike's so strong!" said the river witch.

"Be quiet, all of you," said Aglaonike impatiently. "Let's see what this impostor can do."

Selene just smiled.

Then she reached out to the Moon and plucked a handful of stones from its surface—glowing, white moonstones. She threaded them onto a strand of her hair to make a rope. When she held it next to Aglaonike's rope of white quartz, all the witches had to agree that the moonstones were clearer, brighter, and purer.

Aglaonike was red with rage, but Selene had already moved on to the next task. She went up close to the Moon and whispered something to it. Then the Moon began to glow brighter and brighter: brighter than the stars, brighter than the Sun, and most certainly brighter than Aglaonike's candles.

Aglaonike's hands trembled where she held the Moon's ropes, but she said nothing. Selene smiled once more and reached one hand up to her hair. Then she showed the witches one of the white moonflowers that she wore as a crown. Its petals were pure white and soft as silk; they smelled sweeter than any earthly flower.

The other witches looked at the wilting daisy chain in Aglaonike's hands and had to admit that Selene had won the contest.

At that moment, Aglaonike's ropes of quartz, candles, and daisies all dissolved into moondust. The witch cried out as she felt her magical power leave her. The Moon burst free and sailed up into its usual place in the sky.

Selene left the other witches in peace, and she took no further revenge on Aglaonike. But forever afterward, when the witches of Thessaly gathered under a full moon, they were careful not to boast too much.

Evening Star and Orphan Star

Based on a Caddo Native American tale

Once there was a little boy.

I can't tell you very much else about him. I can't tell you who he was or where he came from. When our story begins, he was already lost. He was unconscious and drifting on the sea waves like a piece of flotsam. There wasn't a ship or shore in sight; just the lost boy, floating along and fast asleep.

After a while, the waves fetched up against an island. It was just about the most desert island you've ever seen. You could walk across it in half a minute. The floor was sandy and dry. There were a few scrubby bushes, and that was it.

But the lost boy didn't know any of this yet. The waves carried him up onto the shore a little way and put him down gently on the wet sand. Then the tide went out, and the waves went away, leaving the boy behind.

It was a very, very long time before he woke up. The sun had moved all the way across the sky, and night had fallen again. The island got very cold at night, and the boy woke up suddenly, shivering.

He stared around him in puzzlement. (He couldn't remember who he was or where he came from, either.) He thought that he should explore the island, but then he discovered that he was terribly thirsty. His legs wobbled, and he couldn't walk very far.

"Excussse me," said a soft voice. "Do you need sssome help?"

The boy looked around wildly. There was no one in sight.

"Sssearch a little lower," said the voice again.

The boy looked at the ground at his feet. Then he crouched down and squinted into the bushes. Sure enough, there was somebody else on the island: a vast green serpent with a horned head.

The serpent opened its jaw in something that might have been a smile.

"Welcome to my isssland," it said. "Would you like sssomething to drink?"

Now, you may be thinking that this serpent was a suspicious character. But the young boy was lost, alone, and very thirsty indeed. He gratefully accepted the serpent's help.

The creature wriggled its long, shimmering body around until there was a small hole in the sand and told the boy to reach inside. Nervously, he put just the tips of his fingers into the hole—and found a cup filled with delicious, fresh, cold water.

"Thank you very much," the boy said to the serpent. Wherever he had come from, they had certainly taught him his manners.

"It'sss my pleasure," said the serpent. "Isss there anything elssse that you need?"

"I think I would like to go home," said the boy, and hesitated. "Only I'm not sure where that is. Getting

off this island might be a start." Then he added, "Not that it's a bad island. I'm sure it's very nice here."

"It isss a good isssland," said the serpent, "it hasss very good viewsss. Ssspectacular for ssstargazing. But of coursse, I will help you again."

The serpent offered to carry the boy across the sea and back to the nearest shore. As soon as he had finished his drink, the boy clambered onto the serpent's back, shuddering slightly at the slippery scales under his hands. Then the serpent wriggled its way to the water's edge and pushed off into the waves.

As soon as they were in the water, the boy realized that this must be a sea serpent. It moved much more easily in the water than on land. It sped through and over the gigantic ocean waves as if it was flying.

The boy, who had been nervous of the serpent a few minutes earlier, began to enjoy the ride. He saw dolphins leaping along in their pods, seabirds startled out of their sleep by the serpent, and hundreds of stars twinkling in the night sky above.

He knew most of the constellations, but there was one star that he didn't know. It burned very brightly, straight ahead of them, and it wobbled and struggled as if it were trying to escape something.

"Look at that!" he said, pointing it out to the serpent. "What a brilliant star! I've never seen that one before."

"What?" said the serpent. "Ssshark! I sssee a ssshark!"

The serpent coiled around on itself and dashed back toward the island. The boy begged and pleaded with it to keep going as they had agreed, but the serpent refused.

"Another night," it said. "It'sss not sssafe. Dangerousss waterssss."

They returned to the island, and the boy spent a chilly night curled up on the wet sand, while the serpent lurked in the bushes. The next day, the serpent agreed that they would attempt the journey again. They set off as soon as the sun had gone down.

"What can you ssssee tonight?" asked the serpent. "I have alwaysss been interested in ssstarsss, myssself."

"It's a beautiful night," said the boy. "I can see that strange bright star again."

The serpent coiled around itself three times in agitation and then lit out straight for the island.

"What are you doing?" cried the boy. "You promised we would keep going this time!"

"I have crampsss," said the serpent, "in my tail."

The next night it was the same. As soon as the boy noticed the bright star, the serpent announced that it thought a storm was coming up.

The night after that, it said the seaweed was too thick to swim through.

The night after that, it shimmied around and said it was fighting off a giant squid, but the boy couldn't see a single tentacle.

By now, he was pretty sure that the serpent was lying. It always came up with an excuse at the same moment: as soon as the bright, trapped star came into view. The boy decided that the next night, he would pretend not to see it. The serpent wouldn't notice for some time, because it kept its head down in the water as it swam.

As usual, the boy and the serpent set off just after dark. He kept it distracted by talking about the birds and the fish he could see.

"No ssstarsss tonight?" asked the serpent.

"Only the usual ones," said the boy cheerfully. "I can't see that strange, bright one today."

The serpent was satisfied and kept swimming. But the boy could see the bright star perfectly well. In fact, it was getting closer and closer and brighter and brighter until he almost thought he could see its shape behind the glow. It looked like the shape of a man.

"But that would be silly," the boy said to himself.

The serpent kept on flowing through the waves. The star came even closer, and the boy's hands tightened on the serpent's back with excitement.

"What isss it?" asked the serpent.

"Oh, nothing," said the boy. "I thought I saw a starfish."

"Up here on the sssurface?" snorted the serpent. "How sssilly. You might as well sssay that you sssaw a ssshark or a sssquid."

The boy realized that the serpent had just admitted it was lying before. But he said nothing and kept his eyes fixed on the star ahead.

By now, it was clear that the star was a man—a shining, bright, star man. He was running toward them over the top of the waves with a furious, determined expression on his face.

The serpent burst up out of the water with an angry screech.

"You ssstupid boy! Why didn't you tell me the ssstar was sssneaking up on us?"

"It's a good thing he did keep quiet!" said the star, in a big, booming voice. "You've kept me trapped here for too long, you horrible old snake!"

"And I'll keep you even longer," hissed the serpent. "For the ressst of time!"

The star drew himself up and closed his eyes in concentration. His light burned even brighter for a second. Then he shot an arrow of light toward the serpent.

The serpent cringed and twisted aside. The waves steamed where the star's arrow landed, but the star was already preparing another attack.

"Jump aside!" he called out to the boy. "Swim back to the island! I'll come and help you afterward."

"Ssstay with me!" urged the serpent. "He'sss dangerousss, I promissse you. Let'sss kill him, and then we'll go home!"

"I don't believe you!" shouted the boy. He dove off the serpent's back and began swimming for the island. He could hear the boom and hiss of the battle behind him. The star was flinging arrows at the serpent as it swirled and splashed in the water. The sea steamed and boiled while the fight raged on.

The boy reached the island and lay panting with exhaustion. He felt miserable. He had been deceived by the serpent all this time—and even now, there was no guarantee that the serpent could be defeated.

But—although he didn't know it yet—the boy had already helped the star win. When the fight started, the serpent hoped that the star would be scared of hurting the boy by accident. So when the boy swam back to the island, he made it easier for the star to attack the serpent with all his might.

The battle went on for some time, but after a while, it seemed to the boy that more of the star's arrows were finding their mark. The serpent still squirmed and thrashed,

but its movements were weaker. Then, with one last, terrible shriek, it was defeated. Its silvery-green body sank to the bottom of the sea.

The star came speeding over the water to the boy.

"We made it!" said the star, landing on the beach with a brilliant smile. The boy felt his clothes drying immediately in its heat.

"What was that thing?" he asked the star.

"That was a sea monster," said the star, frowning. "A few months back, I came a bit too close to Earth, and he caught me. He's stopped me from shining in the right place ever since. I should be up there—" and he pointed far, far into the sky, "showing the other stars when to come out. Now that you've helped set me free, I can finally go home."

"I wish I could go home," said the boy wistfully. "I'm not sure where I came from."

"Hmm," said the Evening Star. "I don't know where you came from either. But I wonder where you might go next?"

"What do you mean?" asked the boy.

"Have you ever thought about becoming a star?"

If you look up at the sky next evening, you will see the Evening Star appear. Look closer, and you might see another star by his side, too. The lost boy found his place in the sky beside his friend, and they are still shining away up there.

HINA and the SHARK

Based on Tongan myths

Somewhere, surrounded by glittering blue seas, there is a lush green island that floats like a gem on the surface of the ocean. A wide reef curves around it, surrounding the island with calm waters that are full of fish. The island is covered with flowers, fruit, and trees; the birds sing all day, and the pigs snuffle their way through the undergrowth.

This is the island where Hina and her family lived. Hina was the youngest, and her parents and her three brothers doted on her. Whenever they went out fishing, they would look for treasures to bring home to her. She filled her room with these delights: the coral that hardened into marble when it left the sea, shells, stones with a hole in the middle (which are especially lucky), sea glass, and mother-of-pearl.

But the presents that Hina liked best were living creatures. Once, her brothers found a tiny baby piglet that had been left behind by its family. Hina fed the piglet and snuggled it and watched it grow up. She could make seabirds fly to her hand and tiny fish swim through her hair.

One day, the whole family went out fishing together. They paddled their canoe out into the bay, safe in the protective arms of the reef. Hina's parents and her brothers set up their fishhooks and waited for a bite, while Hina relaxed in the hot sunshine, looking at the clear blue of the sea and the bright birds flying overhead.

After a while, one of her brothers said "I think there's a big fish nearby. Did you see that shadow pass under the boat?"

"It was just a cloud passing over," said their father.

"No, I definitely saw it!" insisted the boy. "Really big, like a shark."

Hina's mother tutted.

"We don't get sharks inside the reef. And even if we did, they're bad luck. I don't want you trying to catch it."

Then another of Hina's brothers let out a yelp. "I saw it! I saw the shark!"

"Are you sure?"

"As clear as day! I think it was a bull shark."

Everybody was peering over the side of the canoe, trying to catch a glimpse of it.

"I don't like this at all," said Hina's father. "Sharks belong to the gods. What's it doing here?"

"There it goes!" cried out the third brother.

"Let's head back in, quickly now," said Hina's mother. "I don't want this shark coming anywhere near us."

But it was too late. The bull shark—which was only a baby—was snagged on one of the sharp fishhooks.

"It's hurt, the poor thing!" Hina said.

"We'll have to pull it in to take the hook out," said her father briskly. "Everybody—*heave!*"

They brought the shark, gasping and thrashing, onto the canoe. Hina was fascinated by it. Its skin wasn't smooth, the way it had looked in the water, but rough and gritty like sandpaper. Its little black eyes gleamed and flickered.

"He's beautiful," Hina breathed.

"He's dangerous!" said her mother. "We should throw him back right away."

"I want to keep him," said Hina, stubbornly.

The rest of the family exchanged looks. They knew that it was not a good idea to catch a shark. On the other hand, it was not a good idea to argue with Hina. Once she had made her mind up, it was very hard to persuade her out of something.

"I suppose we could dig a channel along the beach," said one of her brothers doubtfully. "So he could swim up and down, but he'd stay close by."

"Exactly," said Hina. "It'll be easy. I'll help!"

The next few weeks passed happily. Each day, Hina would run down to the beach and set off swimming toward her shark. They tumbled through the water, played hide-and-seek through the seaweed, and competed to see who could jump higher out of the water.

But whenever Hina and her family set off in the canoe, the young shark would swim up and down the channel as if it were desperate to join them. Hina's family knew that the shark was supposed to be free, but Hina wouldn't listen to them.

"He likes being near me," she said defiantly.

"No good will come of this," said Hina's mother, "mark my words."

"Hmm," said her father. "The shark belongs to the gods, after all. We can only wait to see what they decide."

The answer from the gods would come sooner than they knew.

A few days later, a strange chill came into the air at sunset. Dark clouds were rolling in across the reef, and they could smell rain on the wind.

"Perhaps it will blow past us," said one of the boys, then jumped in surprise at a huge crack of thunder.

"We'd better get under shelter," said Hina's father grimly. "These night storms are the worst kind. Everybody inside!"

"What about my shark?" asked Hina.

"He'll be just fine in the water," said her mother. "You can't get any wetter when you're already swimming! Come inside now, Hina."

They had barely got inside when the storm broke. Rain came down in sheets, lightning bolts crackled across the dark night sky, and the thunder kept up a steady drumbeat until dawn. The family fell asleep to the sound of huge waves crashing against the shore.

Hina's mother was the first to wake up the next day. She quickly shook everyone else out of their sleep.

"Something's different," she said. "I can hear it. The sea has changed."

They all ran out of the house and went down to the shore. Hina's mother was right. The sea had changed completely. The whole reef had been swept away in the storm, leaving the island at the mercy of the big ocean waves. And the beach where Hina's shark lived was gone.

"He's gone!" sobbed Hina. "My shark is gone! We have to go and look for him!"

Fortunately, there were still a couple of canoes that had not been too badly damaged by the storm. The whole family piled into two boats, and they set out on the rough new seas: Hina and her parents in one canoe and the three brothers in another.

They searched for hours. Hina called out to the shark all the time as they went. Her voice carried far across the water, but it started to seem as if they would never find the little bull shark again.

Then one of the brothers said, "Wait! I think I saw a shadow."

"Where? Where?"

"There!" said Hina's mother. "I saw his fin move!"

They all paddled as hard as they could to catch up with the shark that was skimming through the water ahead of them. But it seemed as if he was teasing them. He would let the canoe get very close—almost close enough for Hina to reach out and touch him—and then he would dash away through the waves.

"Why won't he wait for me?" Hina sobbed.

"Hina," her father said gently, "you have to remember that he's a wild shark. He's grown up now. He wants to live free in the ocean."

"Then so do I!" stormed Hina. "He's my best friend! I'm supposed to be with him!"

The rest of the family looked at each other.

"What do you mean?" her mother asked.

"I like swimming! I like being in the water all day! When my shark came along, I knew that I belonged in the water. I don't want to go home to the island. I want to stay here with him."

Everyone was silent for a while. Hina stared at them stubbornly.

"You know, it's never worked in the past," said one of her brothers. "Trying to change Hina's mind. We can never do it. But the funny thing is, it usually turns out that she was right in the end."

"You swim better than any of us," chimed in another of the brothers. "If anybody can keep up with the sharks, it's you."

Her father sighed deeply.

"You are growing up, just like that little shark. If you really want to live in the ocean, then we have to let you go. Maybe you belong with the sea gods, just like the sharks do."

"So … can I go with him?" Hina asked. "I'll miss you all very much, but I want this more than anything in the world."

"If you're sure, then you should go," her mother said firmly. "But we will always be watching out for you. Don't forget about us."

"I won't!" said Hina. She hugged both her parents and each one of her brothers very tightly. Then she smiled the biggest smile they had ever seen and dived off the side of the canoe.

They watched her flicker through the water, as fast as a shark's shadow. She soon drew level with her friend the bull shark. She threw her arms around its fin—and then the two friends disappeared into the ocean.

The rest of the family sat in silence for a long time, their eyes straining across the water. Eventually, one of the brothers asked, "What happens now?"

"The three of you should head back to the island," their mother said. "The island will still be a good place to live, with a little care. You can rebuild everything."

"What about you?" her children asked.

"We will be keeping an eye on Hina, just as we promised," their father explained. "We can't come home yet. We'll be following her across the seas."

They all hugged again and said their goodbyes. Then the two canoes set off in separate directions: one returning to the island and the other journeying out into the unknown.

Hina's parents followed her across the ocean. They were sad that she couldn't stay with them, but they could see that she was happy. She and the bull shark explored the seven seas and the four corners of the Earth, from the North Pole to the South. The sea gods smiled on them and kept them safe.

The sea gods looked out for Hina's parents, too. They guided their canoe up into the heavens along a rainbow, so that they could travel through the sky and never lose sight of Hina.

You can still see them sailing along up there in the constellation that is called Orion's Belt: two starry figures patiently paddling their canoe.

How Fisher Brought the Sun to Earth

Based on an Ojibwa Native American folktale

Did you know that the world used to be much colder? And I mean much, much, much colder. The land was covered in snow as high as the trees. The sea was full of icebergs as big as mountains. There were not very many people on Earth, but the animals were smart and talkative. They had to be, to survive the cold.

What made the world so cold? Now, there's a question. You see, in those days, there was no spring, no summer, and no autumn. It was always winter. The sun was trapped behind a great, thick wall of dense, white clouds. Its beams couldn't reach the Earth, and the animals on Earth couldn't feel its heat. Everything was dark and chilly.

Can you imagine it? Always winter and never spring! Always nighttime and never day! Always shivering. Never feeling the sun on your face or watching it shine on the grass. The animals who lived at that time were pretty unhappy.

One day, four of them huddled around a campfire in the Ojibwe lands: Fisher, Otter, Lynx, and Wolverine. They were complaining about the cold, as you probably would do in the same situation.

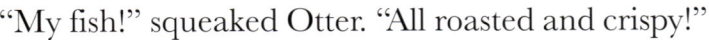

Now before we go on, I must take a moment to tell you about Fisher. There are not many Fishers around these days, so you might not know what he looked like. You must think of a creature that has the deep, snuggly fur of a bear in winter; the fluffy tail and fast movements of a cat; and the clever face of a weasel. Fisher could climb the tallest trees and run across the most powdery snow without a break. The other animals looked up to him because he was so bold.

On this particular occasion, he was sitting and frying big forest mushrooms on the fire. Otter had brought an armful of fish, and Lynx and Wolverine had helped pile up the firewood. They were all looking forward to the feast. But just as it was almost ready, *poof*! A blanket of snow slid off the top of one of the trees and snuffed the fire out.

"My fish!" squeaked Otter. "All roasted and crispy!"

"We spent hours making that fire," snarled Lynx.

"Stupid trees!" said Wolverine. "Always dropping snow on us."

But Fisher just looked thoughtful.

"It's not the trees that are the problem," he said. "They're just as cold as we are, after all. No—the real problem is that it's winter all the time. We need more sunlight."

"How are we going to fix that?" asked Lynx, sarcastically.

"Build a bigger fire!" said Otter.

"Roast the trees!" said Wolverine.

"We'll go up the sky," said Fisher, "and peel the clouds away. The sun is there. We just have to get to it."

It sounded like a very daring plan. But the other animals all trusted Fisher. They knew that he was clever and brave. If he said that there was a way to go up the sky, then chances were that he was right.

They made sure that the ashes of the fire were completely out, then set off on their journey, munching the cold remains of the fish as they went.

Fisher guided them through the frozen forest toward the tallest mountain of all. Its peak reached all the way up into the snow clouds.

"Can we really get all the way up there?" asked Wolverine.

"I'll race you!" said Lynx. The two of them set off at a run for the top of the mountain. Otter trotted along behind, and Fisher followed last of all.

The mountain was hard going. In some places, the snow was so powdery and light that your feet would sink deep into it; in other places, the path was bare rock covered with a deceptive sheen of black ice. Soon, Lynx had to slow her rapid pace, and Wolverine was puffing with effort. Otter kept moving, weaving his way along the path, but even he slipped and slid from time to time. Fisher bounded steadily through the snow behind them all.

Eventually, they reached the top of the mountain. The clouds pressed thickly around them, soaking their fur and beading on their noses.

"Now what?" shivered Wolverine.

"We'll have to jump for it," said Fisher.

Otter went first. He pattered quickly toward the summit, then launched his body upward—but it was no good. He missed the sky and slid back down toward the others on his stomach.

Next, Lynx tried. She started slowly, gathering speed with her long, strong legs as she sprinted forward and leaped into the air. But she, too, missed the sky.

Then Wolverine tried. She dashed up to the tip of the mountain and sprang upward, snapping at the clouds with her teeth. But she, too, fell back to Earth.

Last of all, it was Fisher's turn. His friends stood back to give him a clear path. He began running forward with the sinuous, bouncing run that all Fishers have to this day. Then, at the tip of the mountain, he kicked upward and caught onto the clouds with his

claws. The last thing the other animals saw was his long, bushy tail swinging in the wind … and then he was gone.

Wolverine ran in circles in fright.

"Fisher! Fisher! Where are you?"

Lynx yawned and laid her head down on her paws.

"He made it through the clouds. He'll be back, don't you worry."

"We'll just stay right here and wait for him," said Otter, burrowing comfortably into a nearby snowdrift.

But they would wait a long time to see their friend again.

Fisher had indeed made it through the clouds to the sky beyond. Just at the same time that his friends were wondering where he had gone, he was sitting on top of the snow clouds, gazing around him.

You must remember that in those days, nobody ever saw the sun. Fisher could scarcely believe his eyes. The tops of the clouds were tinted gold and pink with the rosy glow of the sunshine. The sky glowed with a pure blue. And best of all, he could feel the warmth of the sun washing over him. He even steamed slightly as the snow on his fur melted and began to evaporate.

It was better than his wildest dreams.

Fisher wanted to bring the sunlight back to all his friends. He knew that he had to share such a delightful thing with the other animals. So, after sitting on the clouds for a little while and getting his breath back, he got up and began running forward again.

He climbed farther and farther into the sky, looking for a good place to let the sunshine in. At last, he found it. He fastened his sharp little teeth into the clouds and began tearing them back in one long strip, making a window for the sun to shine down on the Earth.

Far below, he could see the mountain summit, with Otter, Lynx, and Wolverine anxiously waiting for him. He waved to them, but it was too far away to call out. He watched in joy as they felt the sunlight reach them. Otter and Wolverine scampered about playing in the heat, and Lynx rolled onto her back like a kitten!

However, although Fisher was very clever, there was one thing that he didn't know. The sky where the sun shone was not an empty space. It was where the Sky People lived—and back then, they didn't want to share the sun with anyone else.

They had seen Fisher climb up through the clouds. They had watched him bathe gratefully in the sun. And then they had seen him tear a strip off the sky to let the sunlight through to Earth.

The Sky People were very angry. They snatched up their weapons and ran to attack Fisher. They rushed toward him with lightning-bolt swords and arrows fletched with feathers from the highest-flying birds.

He began to dodge and weave, running over the snow clouds, still peeling a strip off the clouds as he went. The hole in the sky got bigger and bigger, and Earth got warmer and warmer … and the Sky People got angrier and angrier.

Now there is one more thing that you should know about Fisher. He was very strong, cunning, and fast. Very few of the arrows reached him, and those that did got caught in his thick, wiry fur. But he had one vulnerable point, just under his tail.

He was running speedily away from the Sky People, and the hole in the sky was almost complete, when one of them shot an arrow at just the right place. It pierced through Fisher's hide, and the life began to drain out of him at once. He collapsed onto the clouds and rolled onto his back. The brave, bold, clever, generous Fisher was dead.

Wolverine, Lynx, and Otter had been watching the fight from the top of the mountain. They couldn't

reach the sky themselves, but they had heard the whole thing. Now they began to cry and howl and rail against the Sky People.

"How could you hurt our friend?"

"He was trying to help all the Earth animals!"

"Don't you have enough sunshine to share?"

The Sky People stopped their attack and looked at one another. It was true that the sunlight never ran out; there was more enough to share. It had been selfish of them not to share any light with the creatures on Earth. They began to feel ashamed of themselves.

"Can't you make him better?" wept Otter. "Isn't there anything you can do?"

One of the Sky People walked over to the hole in the sky and dropped down onto the mountain to talk to the little animals.

"I am very sorry," she said. "We should have thought about it before we attacked. But I'm afraid that there's nothing we can do. Once someone is dead, they're dead; they can't come back to Earth."

"But Fisher was a hero," sniffed Wolverine.

"That's true," said the Sky Woman. "I suppose there is one thing we could do."

The Sky People put their heads together. There was a lot of discussion and muttering and gesturing. Then, after asking permission from his friends, they carried Fisher's body gently away.

"What are you going to do with him?" Lynx asked.

"We can't give him back to you on Earth," explained the Sky Woman. "But we do have the power to make him into a star. We'll put him in the sky, just as he was in his finest hour. Every year, he'll walk across the sky to bring the sun out and make the summer. But at the end of summer, he must roll onto his back and travel away again with the sun."

"But the sun will still shine," frowned Otter, "and we'll get to see him for part of the year?"

"Every year," said the Sky Woman, "for the rest of time."

And so, although their hearts were broken, Fisher's friends saw him rise into the sky: a hero made of stars. Even today, if you live in the northern part of the world, you can see him walk across the sky each year to bring warmth and light back to the Earth.

How Thoth Won the Moon

Based on Egyptian myths

Once upon a time, the Moon shone as brightly as the Sun, and the Earth was empty except for the gods. Things were much quieter in Egypt then!

This is how it was. Ra was the sun god, and he was very proud. He didn't want to share the world with anybody else.

There were a few other gods—the sky, the Moon, and so on—but that was all. This small group of gods walked the Universe on their own. No one else was born, nothing changed, and nothing happened.

Although Ra liked this way of things, not everyone was happy. One day, the sky goddess Nut came to see Ra.

"I've been thinking," she said, "if I had children, there would be more gods in the world. Wouldn't that be nice? We've got space for them. They would make the world so much more exciting."

"What sort of thing did you have in mind?" asked Ra.

"Well, they might decorate the Earth with rivers and trees. They might make more animals and people. Then there would be more of us to watch your sunrises and sunsets," she added, hoping that this would flatter Ra.

But the sun god was too proud and jealous.

"Absolutely not," he said, "I forbid it. You will never have children! Not on a single day in the calendar!"

Nut went away crying. Her tears rained down for seven days and seven nights.

The other gods were concerned, but Ra just said, "Leave her alone. She's just in a bad mood. It's not important."

Most of them accepted this explanation and ignored Nut's tears. But one of the gods thought differently.

Thoth was the god of wisdom. Unlike the others, he didn't take Ra's words at face value. He sat down and thought very deeply, while Nut's tears rained down, and then he went to see her.

"Can you tell me what Ra said to you?" he asked. "Maybe I can help."

"He told me that I can't have children— not ever!" sobbed Nut. "Not on a single day in the calendar!"

"Hmm," said Thoth. "And how many days are there in the calendar?"

"Three hundred and sixty," said Nut. "Everybody knows that, Thoth."

"I suppose they do," said the god of wisdom cheerfully. "Even Ra knows that."

He went away whistling, which annoyed Nut very much.

Now you may be wondering to yourself what was going on in Egypt, because today everybody knows that there are 365 days in a year. However, in those days, things were different: the Sun and the Moon shone equally bright, and there were only 360 days in the calendar. This is what gave Thoth an idea.

The next person he went to see was Khonsu, the god of the moon.

In those days, Khonsu was much younger and grander than he is now. He glowed silver and white, as bright as day. He shone so clearly that you couldn't even see the stars at night—they were hidden by his dazzle. He held court in a white marble palace filled with hawks and falcons that flew on errands for him and served as his guards. But however grand he was, he always had time to sit and talk to Thoth.

"Thoth! It's been too long since you came to see me," he greeted him. "What news have you got?"

"Oh, nothing much," said Thoth. "I just felt like playing a game of senet, and you're always my toughest opponent. Do you have time?"

"Always," grinned Khonsu, "but only if you make it interesting. Are we gambling?"

Thoth smiled to himself. This was exactly what he had hoped for.

"Why, certainly," he answered. "If you win, I hand over all my magical powers. And if you lose, I get to take just a tiny portion of your light."

This should have made Khonsu suspicious at once. But you must remember that Thoth was the god of magic and wisdom. All the other gods envied how clever and powerful he was. Khonsu would have risked anything to get his hands on Thoth's magic.

"Done!" he said, and they sat down to play.

I don't know if you have ever played a game of senet. It's a game with ten pieces—five for each player—that move around on a board with 30 squares. It looks a little bit like chess, and the gods used to play it to decide all kinds of bets.

Thoth and Khonsu were the best at senet. Their heads were full of devious moves and tricks. While they sat facing each other across the board, the game pieces clicked back and forth in a complex struggle. But the two gods kept talking all the time.

"You know what I've always liked about senet?" remarked Thoth. "The way it tells

a story. Here, your pawn starts at the beginning of the board. Then she travels forward through her life, until she gets to the end and wins."

"It's a lovely metaphor," said Khonsu, smiling. "Your move."

"But, you know, it got me thinking," continued Thoth, his hand hovering over the next pawn, "how *our* lives never move forward. We're still stuck on square one."

"What do you mean?" asked Khonsu.

"Nothing ever changes. You shine just the same. I do the same spells. None of us ever learns anything new or looks any different or has any children …"

"Children!" said Khonsu, nearly knocking the board over. "I'm not old enough to have children!"

"But some of the gods are," said Thoth calmly. "Nut, for example. She wants children."

"Ra would never allow it," said Khonsu. "Not on a single day in the calendar."

"So I hear," said Thoth. "I win."

Khonsu looked down at the board in amazement. Sure enough, all of Thoth's pawns had crossed the board.

"You trickster!" he laughed. "What do I owe you? A gold cup, was it?"

"Now who's the trickster?" retorted Thoth. "You owe me a portion of your light, as you very well remember."

Khonsu sighed. He did remember, but he had hoped that Thoth would forget.

"How much do you want?" he asked, taking off his headdress, where the silver disk of the Moon sat shining.

"Oh, not much," said Thoth. "About enough for five days of light."

"Five days?" asked Khonsu.

"Yes, five days. Five new days that aren't in the calendar."

Khonsu's eyes grew round with amazement as he realized what Thoth was doing. He was going to make five new days that were not in the calendar, so that Nut could have the children she wanted.

Khonsu winced as he bent the Moon between his hands and snapped off one thin piece. Then he handed it over to Thoth, asking him to take good care of it.

"Of course, I will," said Thoth.

He gave the sliver of Moon to an ibis. The ibis was Thoth's most beloved bird. They flocked to him and were always happy to help him with his magic. The bird held the fragment of Moon carefully in its long, black beak and flew off to put it in the sky.

Then Thoth went to see Nut again.

"Come outside, I have something to show you," he said.

"Go away," said Nut, "I'm busy being miserable."

"I know you are, but you should come outside anyway. I got you a present," said Thoth.

Nut's eyes were still red with tears, but she came outside to see what Thoth had got for her. At first, she couldn't figure out what it was.

"There's nothing here," she said. "What are you talking about?"

"Don't you notice anything?" asked Thoth. "Look! It should be nighttime, but it's day! I made you five extra days."

"Five days that aren't in the calendar," said Nut slowly.

"That's right. Five days that Ra can't control you. Now you can have children, just as you wished."

Nut flung her arms around Thoth's neck and thanked him over and over.

"But how did you do it?" she asked.

"It was just a game of senet," said Thoth, modestly.

It would not be long before Nut's children were born. She had five children—one for each day that Thoth had made for her.

First, there was Osiris. He planted crops all over Egypt and made it a rich, green

land for people to live in. He was Nut's pride and joy, and her sky shone blue for him.

Second, there was Set. He made the desert around Egypt and brought storms over the country. He was the most turbulent of Nut's children, but she loved him just the same.

Third, there was Isis. She healed people when they got sick and kept their ships safe when they sailed up and down the great delta of the Nile river.

Fourth, there was Nephthys. She ruled the night and protected the Egyptian people from harm. It was said that she could breathe out flames to keep attackers away.

Fifth, there was Horus the Elder. He was the chief advisor to the kings and queens of Egypt, because he always saw things clearly and told the truth.

Nut watched over all her children from the sky, and she was happy.

It was just as Thoth had said. Before, the gods were stuck like pawns at the beginning of a game of senet. They never had children or changed or learned anything. When Thoth won the moonlight from Khonsu, he set them all moving around the board.

Nut had her children; that was what she wanted. Thoth learned new powers. Now that he was responsible for five new days, he became the god of time, keeping track of the days and years for all the other gods.

And Khonsu changed. Without the fragment that he had given to Thoth, the Moon was no longer perfectly round. It waxed and waned over the course of the month. Most importantly of all, it shone less bright.

Khonsu's light dimmed. The nights were no longer the same as the days. His palace began to crumble, and his fine clothes began to fray.

But he was happy with the changes in his life. Set free from shining every single night, he was able to explore the new world that Nut's children had made. He had more time to play senet with Thoth. He did not glow so powerfully anymore, but he found new ways to shine.

LINDU and the NORTHERN LIGHTS

Based on a traditional Estonian folktale

This is a story from far above the North Pole, where the wind swoops and crackles with magnetic charges and the clouds are frozen into ice. It is the story of how Lindu, Queen of the Birds, guides them to shelter every winter.

It wasn't always this way. A long, long time ago, Lindu was just a young girl. She was the only child of Ukko, the Sky King, and he loved her dearly.

One day, he came to her and said, "Lindu, you have grown up into a wonderful young woman. You're beautiful, clever, and strong. So I think it's time …"

"Yes, father?" Lindu said excitedly.

"I think it's time … for you to get married!"

"Oh," said Lindu. "Is that all?"

"I thought you'd be more interested," said Ukko.

"I'm not opposed to the idea," said Lindu. "But I want to live a life that's full of excitement and adventures. I'll only get married if I can find someone to have adventures with me."

"I suppose that's fair," said Ukko. "I have some people I'd like you to meet."

Secretly, he was rather worried. This wasn't how he'd expected the conversation to go. It hadn't occurred to him that Lindu might have her own plans.

However, he was confident that she would like the suitors he'd found. He wrote to each one and warned them that they would need to make a good first impression.

"At least one of them is sure to get her attention," he thought. Then he gave three letters to three geese and sent them off to deliver the messages.

The first letter was delivered to the North Star, where he sat on a shining throne above the North Pole. Polaris was an elegant young man who wore white and gold clothes to help him shine as brightly as possible. When the goose arrived with his letter, he stifled a yawn and began to read.

"Oh, dear," he said, "I shall have to see this girl. Fetch my coach! Fetch my horses! And find me ten gifts that a girl would like!"

Polaris' attendants fetched the coach and put six fine brown horses in harness. They showed him ten magnificent gifts of bracelets, necklaces, crowns, and mirrors, which were stowed in the carriage. And then … he sent the carriage away!

You see, the North Star never likes to move. It stays in the same spot, marking the road north. So Polaris sent his carriage to fetch Lindu, rather than going to meet her himself.

Lindu was not impressed. When she tumbled out of the coach after a long journey through the sky, she was tired and disgruntled. She didn't like the gifts, either.

"Welcome to the North Pole," said Polaris, languidly.

"Do you ever leave it?" snapped Lindu.

"Oh, no!" he said in surprise. "I must stay here and shine as much as I can. It's very intensive work."

"Don't you get bored?"

"Bored?" The North Star looked confused. "Do you think I should be zooming around all the time? That sounds very tiring."

Lindu set her teeth and got back in the carriage for the journey home. She said to Ukko:

"I *will not* marry Polaris. You can't have adventures with someone who never goes anywhere."

"Fair enough," said Ukko. "I have a few more candidates up my sleeve."

But secretly, he was still a little worried.

Lindu's next suitor was the Moon, and Ukko was relieved that he came to visit in person. The Moon arrived in a silver carriage drawn by ten brown horses with exquisitely gleaming coats. As he stepped out to meet Ukko and Lindu, he snapped his fingers, and twenty attendants ran forward with twenty gifts. He had brought Lindu moonflowers, moonstones, paintings of the Moon, moon-cheese (which is the finest and sweetest you will ever find), moondust, and fifteen other things to show her the grandeur of his kingdom.

"How delightful," said Lindu politely. "Please, stay with us for a few days."

The Moon stayed with them for a month, and at first, things seemed to be going well. Ukko began to hope that things might work out.

But one day, Lindu came to him with a stern look on her face.

"I *will not* marry the Moon," she said.

"Oh," said Ukko. "What happened this time?"

"His face keeps changing!" Lindu said. "Haven't you noticed? He was thin when he arrived. Then he got fatter and fatter. Then he started to get thin again—and today

he's disappeared completely. No, father. I can't have adventures with someone who's changing his face all the time. I need someone reliable."

Ukko sighed.

"Of course, my love. But don't worry: I have one more suitor for you to meet."

The final suitor on Ukko's list was the Sun. He made the grandest entrance of all.

He came dashing up to the palace in a coach made of solid gold. It was drawn by twenty horses with shining red-gold coats. Thirty more horses followed behind, each carrying panniers filled with gold and precious gems.

The Sun jumped down from his carriage and smiled a glowing smile at Lindu.

"Would you like to go for a drive?" he asked her.

"An adventure!" cried Lindu, clapping her hands. "Yes, of course!"

She spent the whole day driving around with the Sun in his carriage with thirty golden horses. They went out again the next day, and the next, and the next.

But on the fifth day, she came to see Ukko. His heart sank when he saw the expression on her face.

"Father …" she began.

"Let me guess," sighed Ukko. "You will not marry the Sun?"

"He follows the same path every single day!" she said. "I can't have adventures with someone who does the same thing every day."

"Well, my dear," said Ukko, "it is your decision. I'll send the Sun home."

Both Lindu and Ukko thought that was the end of that. She had met three suitors, and she didn't like any of them.

Then, one day, Ukko woke up to a great clattering and chiming and clopping outside his palace window at dawn. He went over to the window and poked his head out to see what was happening.

An enormous coach stood in front of the palace, carved from a single flawless diamond. A thousand milk-white horses stood in harness before it, in rows of four. And behind that diamond coach came another, just as large, filled with silver and pearls.

"Lindu! Lindu!" the Sky King called out. "Wake up! I think you have another suitor!"

Lindu came downstairs yawning. When she saw the diamond coach, she stopped and rubbed her eyes. When she noticed the thousand white horses, her mouth dropped open. When she saw the silver and pearls, she almost fainted.

And then she saw the fourth suitor, who took her breath away.

The Northern Lights came out of his diamond coach and strolled up the palace steps toward Lindu and her father. He was stunningly beautiful. A thousand lights played in his hair, and his eyes were as deep as the ocean. The clouds and the stars shimmered for joy when they saw him.

"Father," Lindu whispered in Ukko's ear, "I think I *will* marry this one."

Lindu and the Northern Lights spent the whole day together, talking and laughing as they danced through the sky. He promised to come back the next day. He surprised her with another carriage, this time made of the finest rose quartz, filled with rubies and pulled by black horses. His hair flickered and blazed with different hues than the day before.

"Oh, this is wonderful!" said Lindu. "Every day you go somewhere new, wear new clothes, and have new horses!"

The Northern Lights smiled and promised to come back again the next day.

But, although Lindu sat on the palace steps from dusk until dawn waiting for him, he did not come back the next day. Or the next. Or the next.

On the fifth day, he finally came back. This time the coach was sapphire, the gems were emeralds, and the horses were white.

"Where have you been?" asked Lindu.

"Oh, here and there," he said lightly. "I had important things to do."

Lindu was upset, but she bit her tongue and tried to enjoy the day. After that, the Northern Lights was missing for four days before he came back. Then only two days. Then five days at a time.

Lindu began to look sad and timid. She drifted around the palace silently, only cheering up when the Northern Lights decided to drop in. Every time he visited, he would promise Lindu that things were going to change, that he would only be busy for a little while longer, but then he would disappear again.

Ukko watched her, and he was very worried indeed. He began to realize that there were worse things than Lindu not getting married.

Lindu announced that she was going to go down to Earth and watch out for the Northern Lights in the sky. Ukko hoped that the move would be good for her, but she spent the days weeping until new rivers ran over the Earth. Winter came, and the waters became icy and dangerous. Lindu kept crying.

Eventually, Ukko took matters into his own hands. He ordered the birds to bring Lindu back to his sky palace.

"Listen to me, my darling daughter," he said. "You *will not* marry the Northern Lights. You can't have adventures with someone who leaves you in the lurch like this."

The birds hopped around Lindu, comforting her and offering her berries to eat.

"But I love him!" she said.

"I'm not sure that you do," said Ukko thoughtfully. "I think that you love having adventures. But you don't need the Northern Lights to do that."

He looked at the birds clustering around their feet.

"In fact, I think I might have a job for you."

"I don't want to meet anymore suitors," warned Lindu.

"Certainly not!" said her father. "Look at all these little birds. It's too cold for them here in winter, and they don't know how to find their way south. If I made a path in the stars, could you lead them there and bring them back when summer comes?"

Lindu gazed at Ukko in amazement, then smiled and hugged him.

"Will there be adventures?" she asked.

To this day, Lindu is responsible for guiding the birds from the north to the south each year. That's why, in Estonia, they call the Milky Way Linnutee—the Bird's Way. Wrapped in a warm cloak of feathers, she speeds through the stars, tumbling down byways, visiting new countries, and having endless adventures.

Sometimes, the Northern Lights glimmers across her path, and she gives him a friendly wave. But she won't be fooled again.

The MAN WHO MADE the SUN

Based on a Diné Native American story

Once, a long, long time ago, say the Diné people, the Universe had just been made. The Holy People had found a great dark space, and they had filled it with the Earth and the sky. But it was always nighttime. They couldn't see what they had made.

That wasn't the only problem. Because there were no stars, there was no way to navigate north, east, south, or west. Because there was no Sun, there were no seasons or hours, and everybody had to blunder around in the dark.

The Holy People realized that this was going to be a problem.

"Let's start by making the Sun," suggested the First Woman. "Once we have a Sun, then things will be much easier. We can start organizing the world from there."

The other Holy People all agreed. They started looking around for something that could be a Sun. They thought about using fire and fish scales and drops of water and clouds and all kinds of other things, but none of them shone brightly enough.

Then, as all the Holy People stood around wondering what to do, a strange young man appeared. He wasn't one of them. They'd never seen him before.

He came walking out of the mountains as if he had always been there. He walked until he stood right in the middle of the crowd of Holy People.

"I can help you make a Sun," he said.

He reached into his pocket and pulled out a big, round piece of turquoise. Its blue-green surface shimmered and flashed in the darkness of the new world.

"We will put all the light in here," he said, "but first, it needs to become stronger."

He asked the Holy People to bring all their treasures to him. They laid everything out on a soft buckskin: white shells, pink shells, spotted shells, shiny pieces of black jet, blades of obsidian, fragments of coral in all the shades of the rainbow, rubies, emeralds, sapphires, diamonds, quartz, carnelians, tigereyes, jade, amethysts, peridots, garnets, alexandrites, aquamarines, tourmalines, topazes, and precious stones of every kind!

Heaped up on the buckskin, the gems flashed and glittered so brightly that the Holy People had to shield their eyes.

"Wait," said the young man. "It's not finished yet."

He crouched down next to the buckskin and began to pick up the gems one by one. He would examine each stone carefully, turning it from side to side to check for any flaws—and then, when he was satisfied that it was perfect, he would put the gem into the big piece of turquoise.

As he worked, the turquoise grew bigger and rounder and brighter. It glowed with all the treasure inside it until it shed light over all the Holy People and the land as far as the mountains. But still, the young man kept picking up gems, examining them, and adding them to the new Sun.

He began to talk to the Holy People as he worked.

"This stone will be called One Who Travels In Daytime," he said, "because the Sun will travel across the sky every day. It will light up the whole world with everything you have put inside it: your riches, your generosity, and your love. The people on Earth will tell stories about it and talk about it as if it is one of them."

This impressed the Holy People very much. They nodded and gasped at how bright the Sun had grown, and some of them even found a few more gems to put down on the buckskin.

"I have a suggestion," said the First Man. "If the Sun is going to shine on the Earth people, and they will tell stories about it, then I think the Sun should be like them. I mean, it should look like them, and it should be able to understand them."

The strange young man scratched his head.

"What a funny idea," he said. "I hadn't thought of that."

The Holy People crowded around the turquoise Sun to give it their gifts of humanity. They whispered to it about love, hope, knowledge, kindness, and bravery. To make up the balance, they also taught the Sun about anger, fear, and sadness. All their complicated feelings rippled into the Sun. It sparkled and flashed even brighter.

Then they began to play with the Sun, like children playing with salt dough. They pinched and pulled at the light to stretch it out into the shape of a person, until it had two arms, two legs, and a head. But however hard they tried, it never looked quite like a human shape—it was more like a star, with a round middle and sharp points.

They even drew a face on the head point of the star, with two eyes, two ears, a nose, and a mouth.

"There!" said First Woman. "Now the Sun looks like people."

"It will shine even brighter because it understands them," said the First Man.

The strange young man who had brought them the turquoise just shrugged.

"Let's see how it looks once it's fired up," he said. "It looks bright now, but it has to be strong enough to make the whole world light."

He asked the Holy People to bring him some of the First Fire. He picked up the torch without even wincing, though the fire burned hot and bright. The strange young man carried the torch over to the Sun and blew, sending the flames leaping out toward

the Sun until they had caught. The entire star filled with the shimmering light and heat of a burning fire, reflected and magnified a thousand times by all the precious gems inside it. The young man stepped back and watched the flames.

The Holy People cheered and clapped. They had made a beautiful Sun.

They could feel its warmth on their faces, bathing them in luxurious heat. They could feel it all the way down to their toes. They could feel it almost burning.

Then they realized that they really were burning. They had made such a good, powerful Sun that it was burning up everything around it!

The star was too bright to look at now and they couldn't even see its smiling face. The ground underfoot grew hot and red, like lava. The plants were dry and crisp. The rivers and seas began to steam. The Holy People themselves cowered from the flames.

"We have to move the Sun!" they cried. "It's going to burn the whole world up!"

They had to think fast. Where could they put the Sun so that it would light the world—without destroying it?

"What if we put it on a high, high mountain?" said one of the Holy People.

But as soon as they had rolled the Sun up the mountain together and balanced it on the summit, the stones of the mountain began to melt, and the Sun rolled back down again.

"What if we call up a strong wind to blow the Sun around?" said another.

But when they called up the wind, it burned and stung them with heat. It blew the Sun's flames around even worse than before.

"What if we put it at the bottom of the sea, so it could shine upward?" suggested another.

But as soon as the Sun touched the water, the sea began to boil and spit, evaporating instantly in the Sun's path.

"What if we plant trees all around it to make shade?" said another.

But the trees burned up in seconds and covered the sky with black, choking smoke.

"We need to put it far away from the Earth," said another of the Holy People. "Let's pin it to the sky, where it's out of reach."

When the Sun was in the sky, the heat lessened, and the Holy People sighed with relief. But because the Sun was fixed in one place, half the planet was left cold and dark. It was still nighttime for half the world.

"This will never do," said the First Woman, despairingly. "The Sun has to be far away, but it needs to shine on the whole Earth. It's too heavy to move, but it can't stay in one place. What are we going to do?"

They all looked at the strange young man for guidance. He had seemed so confident as he gathered their treasures together, filled up the Sun, and set it alight. While they had rushed around trying to find a place to put the Sun, he had waited calmly with his arms folded.

Now he stepped forward and spoke again.

"First Woman is right. This is a tricky problem to solve. The Sun must keep moving all the time. It must vary its distance from the Earth. It must be close enough to keep us warm, but far away enough that it can't hurt anyone. It must make the hours, the days, and the seasons."

He paused as the Holy People muttered in discontent. What he was suggesting sounded impossible.

"There is only one way to do this," he said. "Someone must carry the Sun through the sky. The Sun will be One Who Travels In Daytime, just like I told you."

"But who will carry it?" all the Holy People cried.

One by one, they came up to the Sun and tried their luck. The First Woman tried

to lift it, but it burned her hands. The First Man tried to pick it up, but it was too heavy. Coyote tried to push the Sun along with his paws, but it burned him, too.

At last, all the Holy People had tried to carry the Sun, and all had failed. Only the strange young man was left, still standing calmly and watching them.

"Please," said the First Man, "won't you carry the Sun for us?"

The young man looked at the ground. Then he looked at all the Holy People. Then he looked at the Sun. Then he looked at the sky.

Then he said, "I can carry the Sun across the sky each day. But I have a price."

"Name it!" growled Coyote. "We want to get this thing out of here!"

The young man sighed.

"Until now, the people on Earth have been immortal. They live forever. But if you ask me to carry the Sun, then I will take one life each day. That will sustain me as I carry the Sun."

The Holy People looked at one another. This was a hard bargain. The Sun would mean warmth, light, and life for the world—but at the price of a life, every single day.

First Woman stepped forward.

"We accept your price," she said sadly. "We will miss the people that you take. But the Earth will be green and full of life. More people will be born, and they will always be grateful for your sunshine."

The young man nodded. He walked over to the Sun and hoisted it onto his back in one smooth movement, as if it weighed nothing. Then he settled it into place and began to walk slowly into the sky, step by step.

The Holy People sighed in relief as the fierce heat of the Sun lessened. The farther away that the young man walked, the better it was. As the Sun's light moved across the Earth, the hours passed, the day turned into night, and the seasons came around.

The price that the young man had asked was very high and the Holy People grieved for each life that he took. But the First Woman was right. For every life that the young man took, more people were born. And they were always grateful for the sunshine.

The SEVEN SISTERS and the BEAR

Based on a Kiowa Native American folktale

Once there were seven Kiowa sisters. When the first sister was born, their grandmother said, "She looks like an adventurer to me."

"People will be telling stories about her one day, no doubt," agreed their grandfather.

When the next sister was born, their grandfather said:

"This is another adventurer, you mark my words."

"She has that starry-eyed look about her," nodded their grandmother.

When the third sister was born, she looked like an adventurer, too. So did all the other sisters.

So their parents decided to name them First, Second, Third, Fourth, Fifth, Sixth, and Seventh to make it easier for the storytellers later on.

"Oh, those storytellers will need all the help they can get with those girls," said their grandmother.

"Bound to," agreed their grandfather.

The seven girls grew up to be brave, strong, and the best of friends. Each morning, they would set off to explore, with First carrying Seventh and all the other sisters holding hands, so that no one got lost.

They swam in the long, muddy river like otters and climbed trees as fast as squirrels. In the evenings, they would sit around the fire and listen to their grandmother's stories while the birds sang their goodnight songs overhead.

But whatever time of day and wherever they wandered, there were some animals that they knew to avoid.

In that part of the country, there were many grizzly bears. Each one stood taller than a grown man, with claws as long as your hand and teeth that could grind your bones like a millstone.

Now the thing about grizzly bears is that they have two sides.

In summer, grizzly bears are fat and sleepy. They're stuffed full of salmon and berries. The little girls would always hear them coming in plenty of time.

Once they're as round as a barrel, grizzly bears go to sleep for the winter. They sleep and sleep and sleep, until all those fresh salmon and tasty berries are just a distant memory. And in spring, they wake up with a hunger like you've never felt.

Grizzly bears in spring are skinny, sneaky, and nasty, and they'll eat anything that walks past their den. Which is exactly what First, Second, Third, Fourth, Fifth, Sixth, and Seventh did one fine morning at the beginning of spring.

The biggest bear that ever was, was curled up inside his den, surrounded by nice crunchy leaves and warm earth, when he smelled something outside. His nose twitched and his ears flickered. Then slowly, very slowly, he opened one eye.

One—two—three—four—five—six—no, *seven* little girls, walking right past his den.

Slowly, very slowly, the bear wriggled his way outside and stood up to stretch.

The girls stared open-mouthed. He was nearly as tall as the pine trees.

Seventh began to cry. Sixth began to whimper. Fifth said, "I'm not scared!" but her voice wobbled. Fourth gulped. Third trembled. Second wept just one tear. And First bit her lip and looked the bear right in the face.

"It looks like we're having an adventure, girls," she said. "We'd better start running."

She hitched the baby up on her hip, grabbed Second's hand, and took off at a sprint. Her sisters followed close behind, holding hands tightly.

The bear yawned. He roared as loud and long as a rumble of thunder. Then he slammed his paws down on the ground and gave chase. The girls were fast, but the bear was faster.

"This won't do," said First. "Second, carry Fifth! Third, carry Sixth! Fourth, you can do it!"

Fourth was red in the face, but she set her mouth into a hard line of determination. Her legs pumped and her arms swung, and she ran just as fast as her sisters.

They could hear the bear pounding behind them. The earth shook where his feet fell, and the wind whistled through his fur. And he kept running faster and faster.

"We can't keep this up," panted Second, "we need some help. Trees! Bushes! Grass! Flowers! Won't you help us?"

"Yes, please help!" chimed in Sixth.

The plants of the forest had been watching the whole time. They liked bears, but they didn't approve of them eating little girls.

So the grass and the rushes and the ivy that snaked around the trees reached out and snatched at the bear's paws. They set trip wires for him and tied knots around his toes. They even laid thorns in his path, which filled his paws with as many spikes as a cactus.

But it was no good—the bear kept running. And in answer to his thunderous roar, other bears came out of their dens to see what was going on. When they shuffled their way out into the sunlight, the first thing they saw was the seven girls, running as fast as they could. The other bears joined in the chase.

"We're going from bad to worse," said Third, wiping the sweat from her face. "Who else could help us? Wind, are you there? Will you blow for us?"

"Blow, wind, blow!" shouted Fifth.

The wind knew the girls from many days out in the sunshine. It loved to play with their hair and make the beads on their dresses jingle.

It had nothing against bears, but it didn't like to see its friends upset. So the wind huffed and puffed at the bears, buffeting them with breezes and making their eyes water.

But it's almost impossible to stop a grizzly bear that has decided what it wants for dinner. So, however hard the wind blew, the bears just kept running faster and faster.

They were beginning to surround the girls, driving them out of the forest and toward a long, twisting river. The seven sisters were exhausted as they stumbled over the tree roots and rocks.

"We're running out of space," sobbed Fourth. "The river's in the way!"

"We need more help," puffed Second. "Remember grandmother's stories. You always get a third chance in the stories."

"That's right," gasped Second. "The third person you talk to is always the most helpful. Who else do we know around here?"

"The land!" said Fourth. "We can ask the land for help! Oh, Earth, can't you protect us?"

"The bears are getting closer!" shrieked Third.

At first, it seemed like there was no answer to Fourth's plea. But then one little pebble beside her foot started to tremble and roll up the valley, away from the river.

"Look at that," said Fifth.

"Can you hear it?" asked Sixth.

"Go!" said baby Seventh, clapping her hands together.

There was an enormous rocking and rumbling as the whole land came to the girls' aid. Dust, dirt, gravel, and stones rolled together like a landslide running backward.

Behind them, the girls could hear the bears' feet, hammering as hard and fast as their heartbeats. The biggest bear roared, and all the other bears took up the call, until the trees shook and the water in the river seethed.

There were hundreds of bears now, all running straight for the seven sisters. And as they ran, they got more and more hungry.

The plants fell back as the bears left the forest. The wind gave up its blowing, and dropped to a small, miserable breeze stroking the sisters' hair.

"I'm sorry! I'm sorry!" it whispered in their ears.

But the land had not abandoned them.

The earth and rocks and river stones kept piling up beneath the sisters' feet. The girls wobbled and waved their arms for balance as the land lifted them up. The circle of ground where they stood began to grow straight up like a tree trunk.

By now, the bears had circled them completely, growling ferociously. They swiped at the rocks with their sharp claws.

First tightened her grip on the baby and shouted, "We're not scared of you! We're the seven adventuring sisters!"

"The land is on our side," joined in Second. "You'll never get us!"

"The wind and the plants, too," agreed Third. "Go home, bears!"

"Give up! Give up! Give up!" chanted Fourth, Fifth, and Sixth.

"Go away!" shouted Seventh.

But the bears were long past listening.

"Please don't let us down now, Earth," whispered First into the baby's hair. She was trying to be brave in front of her sisters, but she was secretly scared.

The land kept pushing upward into the sky, higher and higher, away from the bears. The wind dropped as the land rose beyond the belt of clouds, carrying the seven sisters higher than any human had ever been.

They could still hear the bears roaring far below and scraping their claws into the soft young rock. They scratched and stabbed as they tried to get a foothold to climb after the girls.

But it was no good. The bears left deep claw marks all around the mountain, but they could not climb it.

The girls began to forget their fear and to look around them.

"I can see all of the long river!" cried out First.

"I can see where the mountains start!" said Second.

"I can see the ocean all around the land!" said Third.

"I can see places that no one's ever explored before!" said Fourth.

"I can see whales!" said Fifth.

"And elephants!" said Sixth.

"Snow!" said Seventh.

Their new mountain kept on rising until they could see the whole Earth laid out at their feet. The sky was cool and dark, and they could feel the first tingles of starlight bathing their skin.

Still, the mountain didn't stop. The seven adventurers laughed in excitement and delight as they kept rocketing toward the Milky Way. The other stars reached out shining hands to greet them and pulled them up to find their seats in the galaxy.

Down on Earth, the bears got tired. They had raged and scrambled and gnashed their teeth, but the mountain was still as solid and unclimbable as ever. They slowly began the long trudge back to their own homes.

The seven sisters are still twinkling in the sky today. You can see them, if you look—although you'll need a telescope to see Seventh, because she's the smallest. Every year in October, when the bears go to sleep, the sisters come out to shine. But they go away adventuring every April, before the bears wake up.